**Young Writers** 2005 POETRY COMPETITION

# Playground Poets

Let your cre...

ode
limerick
haiku
rhyme

## Gloucestershire
Edited by Gemma Hearn

**Young Writers**

First published in Great Britain in 2005 by:
Young Writers
Remus House
Coltsfoot Drive
Peterborough
PE2 9JX
Telephone: 01733 890066
Website: www.youngwriters.co.uk

All Rights Reserved

© Copyright Contributors 2005

SB ISBN 1 84602 132 4

# Foreword

Young Writers was established in 1991 and has been passionately devoted to the promotion of reading and writing in children and young adults ever since. The quest continues today. Young Writers remains as committed to the fostering of burgeoning poetic and literary talent as ever.

This year's Young Writers competition has proven as vibrant and dynamic as ever and we are delighted to present a showcase of the best poetry from across the UK. Each poem has been carefully selected from a wealth of *Playground Poets* entries before ultimately being published in this, our thirteenth primary school poetry series.

Once again, we have been supremely impressed by the overall high quality of the entries we have received. The imagination, energy and creativity which has gone into each young writer's entry made choosing the best poems a challenging and often difficult but ultimately hugely rewarding task - the general high standard of the work submitted amply vindicating this opportunity to bring their poetry to a larger appreciative audience.

We sincerely hope you are pleased with our final selection and that you will enjoy *Playground Poets Gloucestershire* for many years to come.

# Contents

**Beaudesert Park School**

| | |
|---|---|
| Georgia Miles (10) | 1 |
| Rebecca Raby Smith (9) | 1 |
| Thomas Hillman (9) | 2 |
| William Reid (9) | 2 |
| Edward Rankin (9) | 3 |
| Alicia Muir (9) | 3 |
| Rosa Schofield (9) | 4 |
| Robert O'Malley (7) | 4 |
| Xan Somerset (9) | 5 |
| Freddie Waller (9) | 5 |
| Augusta Puckett (8) | 6 |
| Jessica Priest (8) | 6 |
| Katherine Dauncey (11) | 7 |
| Freddie Wyld (9) | 7 |
| Clemmie Melvin (8) | 8 |
| Camilla Purves (8) | 8 |
| Rachel Smith (11) | 9 |
| Hermione Russell (10) | 9 |
| Hector Millar (10) | 10 |
| Dominic Barrington (10) | 10 |
| Sebastian Chater-Davies (10) | 11 |
| Alexander Ferrigno (10) | 11 |
| Michael Young (9) | 11 |
| Laura Gordon Lennox (10) | 12 |
| Isabella Boscawen (10) | 12 |
| Tom Dyson (10) | 13 |
| Freddie Clarke (9) | 13 |
| Katie Burridge (10) | 14 |
| Oliver Gardner (11) | 15 |

**Bishops Cleeve Primary School**

| | |
|---|---|
| Holly Bartlett (11) | 15 |
| Paul Lennon (11) | 16 |
| David McNair (11) | 16 |
| Charlotte White (10) | 17 |
| Yasmin Baig (10) | 17 |
| Gabriella Large (11) | 18 |
| Jade Musto (10) | 18 |

| | |
|---|---|
| Grace Baker  (11) | 19 |
| Megan Sweeney  (11) | 19 |
| Sophie Smith  (11) | 20 |
| David Pinco  (10) | 20 |
| Emily Giles  (10) | 21 |
| Jacob Wilkes  (11) | 21 |
| Gareth Jones  (10) | 22 |
| Amy Daglish  (11) | 22 |
| Jason Andrews  (11) | 23 |
| Joshua Barrett  (10) | 23 |
| Charlotte Holden  (11) | 24 |
| Nathan Webb  (10) | 25 |
| Bethan Reynolds  (10) | 25 |
| Alastair Wade  (11) | 26 |
| Emily Stone  (10) | 26 |
| George Curr  (10) | 27 |
| Megan Frost  (10) | 27 |
| Jack Watts  (10) | 28 |
| Daisy Green  (10) | 28 |
| Jessica Belcher  (10) | 29 |
| Lee Parry  (10) | 29 |
| Ben Carson  (10) | 30 |
| Lauren Dix  (11) | 30 |
| Dominic Evans  (10) | 31 |
| Roxanne Blake  (11) | 31 |
| Penny Sparrow  (10) | 32 |
| Gareth Lee  (10) | 32 |
| Neil Bell  (10) | 33 |
| Sam Mitchell  (11) | 33 |
| Sara Gazzal  (10) | 34 |
| Emily Beuzelin  (10) | 35 |
| Francesca Baillie  (10) | 35 |
| Chloe Webb  (11) | 36 |

**Bledington Primary School**

| | |
|---|---|
| Harry Notman  (9) | 36 |
| Lee Coles  (11) | 36 |
| Ben Pocock  (10) | 37 |
| Eira Walling  (11) | 37 |
| Toby Taylor  (9) | 38 |
| Hayley Jarvis  (10) | 38 |

    Edina Morris  (9)      39
    Toni Wilton  (9)      39
    Becky Pearson  (8)      40

**Cam Hopton CE Primary School**
    Ellen Lockstone  (9)      40
    Elizabeth Grimshaw  (8)      41
    Alice Clarke  (9)      41
    Megan Hambling  (8)      42
    Zoe Latuszka  (9)      42
    Cara Froggatt  (9)      43
    Kane Loveridge  (9)      43

**Deerhurst & Apperley CE Primary School**
    Lucy Topham  (8)      43
    Katie Atkinson  (11)      44
    Hannah Street  (9)      44
    Hannah Stephens  (10)      45
    Isabella Bourne  (10)      45
    Roshin Ono  (9)      46
    Luke Ridal  (9)      46
    Charlie Wiseman  (10)      46
    Amie Booth  (9)      47
    Robert Tattersall  (11)      47
    Lillie Stacey  (7)      47

**Ellwood Community Primary School**
    Rebecca Smith  (10)      48
    Rhiannon Thomas  (11)      48
    Amy Wallace  (10)      49
    Lotti Davies  (11)      49
    Bethan Harper  (10)      50
    Amy Albury  (10)      50
    Georgina Jury  (10)      51
    Jack Smith  (11)      51
    Ryan Hollis  (10)      52
    Joseph Stevenson-Challice  (9)      52
    Kieran Williams  (10)      53
    Thomas Gwilliam  (10)      53
    Conor Burris  (9)      54

| | |
|---|---|
| Damian Farr  (11) | 54 |
| James Hawkins  (8) | 55 |
| Jack Neale  (9) | 55 |
| Sophie Cotterell  (9) | 55 |
| Charlotte Wells  (10) | 56 |
| Emily Jones  (9) | 56 |
| Bridie Downey  (9) | 56 |
| Thomas Rushton  (8) | 57 |
| Zoe Pendrey  (10) | 57 |
| Thomas Brown  (9) | 57 |
| Grace Paddock  (9) | 58 |
| Ben Morse  (10) | 58 |
| Fiona Bott  (9) | 58 |
| Rachel Stephenson  (9) | 59 |
| Tori Maddock  (8) | 59 |
| Jack Akers  (10) | 59 |
| Jack Edmunds  (10) | 60 |
| Liam Jones  (9) | 60 |
| Sam Hatton  (11) | 60 |
| Jessica Downham  (10) | 61 |
| Marcus Partridge  (11) | 61 |
| Melissa Stephens  (9) | 62 |
| Jamie Button  (10) | 62 |
| Reece Leigh  (9) | 62 |
| Joshua Goldstien  (10) | 63 |
| Thomas Winmill  (9) | 63 |

### English Bicknor CE Primary School

| | |
|---|---|
| Jessica Palmer  (9) | 63 |
| Alice Blakemore  (10) | 64 |
| Charlotte Pomeroy  (9) | 64 |
| Lucy Davies  (10) | 64 |
| Josh Baynham  (10) | 65 |
| Jack Reed  (10) | 65 |
| Guy Meredith  (10) | 65 |
| Becky Hone  (10) | 66 |
| Matthew Jackson  (10) | 66 |
| Callum Moore  (10) | 67 |
| Ainsley Robbins  (9) | 67 |
| Laceyjay Wells  (11) | 67 |
| Sam Evans  (10) | 68 |

| | |
|---|---|
| Charlotte Butcher (8) | 68 |
| Bethany Cooper (8) | 68 |
| Harley Adams (9) | 69 |
| Sarah Toomer (11) | 69 |
| Tom Barnett (10) | 69 |
| Jeremy Hale (10) | 70 |
| Amber Jenkins (10) | 70 |
| Jack Powell (9) | 70 |
| Catherine Larcombe (10) | 71 |
| Zak Williams (11) | 71 |

**Foxmoor CP School**

| | |
|---|---|
| Ashleigh Phelps (10) | 71 |
| Janneke Bax-Pratt (8) | 72 |
| Kirsty Lawrence (9) | 72 |
| Sophie Davis (8) | 72 |
| Kiera Yam (9) | 73 |
| Regan Garraway (8) | 73 |
| Kacey Garraway (10) | 74 |
| Samantha Haughton (8) | 74 |
| Charlotte Cowley (9) | 75 |
| Molly Bale (10) | 75 |
| Alys Chitty (9) | 76 |
| Ellena Brown (9) | 76 |
| Jordan Grant (8) | 77 |
| Charis Wyatt (9) | 77 |
| Jefferson Thomas (10) | 77 |
| Aiesha Williams (8) | 78 |
| Zoe Smith (8) | 78 |
| Sam Coates (9) | 78 |
| Lianne Burnell (8) | 79 |
| Danielle Berry (9) | 79 |
| Adam Gloyne (8) | 79 |
| Rowan Duval-Fryer (9) | 80 |
| Victoria Cullen (9) | 80 |
| Alice Samways (10) | 81 |

**Hopelands School**

| | |
|---|---|
| Rachael Boddington (10) | 81 |
| Emily Walker-Smith (11) | 82 |
| Lydia Gray (10) | 82 |

Emily Ham  (8)     83
Alice Lord  (8)     83
Alice Barber  (9)     84
Grace Barber  (10)     84
Siobhan Bradburn  (10)     85
Alice Bloomer  (8)     85
Tom O'Dell  (11)     86

## Kempsford CE Primary School
Emily Hepworth  (9)     86
Alex Britt  (7)     87

## Kingswood Primary School
Giselle Failes  (11)     87
Olivia Harper  (10)     88
Polly Clare-Hudson  (9)     88
Michael Rowe  (10)     89
Katie Smith  (10)     89
Lottie Aldridge  (9)     89

## Kitebrook House School
Lucy Dowling  (10)     90
Antonia Dalivalle  (10)     91
Pandora Fowles  (10)     91
Henrietta Trevelyan  (10)     92
Isobel Styler  (9)     93
Chloe O'Kane  (9)     94
Imogen Gloag  (9)     94
Matilda Jacobs  (8)     95
Francesca White  (9)     95
Polly Hughes  (10)     96
Charlotte Mills  (10)     97
Piera Van de Wiel  (10)     98
Lara Fenton  (10)     99
India Case  (10)     100
Emily Liggins  (10)     101
Courtney Ferguson  (9)     102
Isobel Kenny-Herbert  (10)     102
Bunny Cockerton-Airy  (8)     103
Lottie Carron  (10)     103

| | |
|---|---|
| Lucy Sloane  (10) | 104 |
| Madeleine Allardice  (10) | 104 |
| Ingrid Straume-Brown  (11) | 105 |
| Helen Stewart  (9) | 105 |
| Lucy Colquhoun  (11) | 106 |
| Georgia Wood  (9) | 107 |
| Isabella Grive  (8) | 108 |

**Nailsworth CE Primary School**
| | |
|---|---|
| Martha Hicks  (10) | 109 |
| Liam Close  (10) | 109 |

**Northleach CE Primary School**
| | |
|---|---|
| Pippa Welch  (10) | 110 |
| Emily Creed  (10) | 110 |
| Stephanie Powell  (11) | 111 |
| Nicholas Basson  (11) | 111 |
| Cait Bleakley  (10) | 112 |
| Imogen Deacon  (11) | 112 |
| Paige Yates  (11) | 113 |
| Rosemary Webb  (11) | 113 |
| Jamie Fisher  (11) | 114 |
| Ashley Nash  (11) | 114 |
| Shelley Larner  (10) | 115 |
| Jennifer Powell  (11) | 116 |

**St David's Primary School, Moreton-in-Marsh**
| | |
|---|---|
| Raffles Moulder  (10) | 116 |
| Gary Luker  (11) | 117 |
| Zara Oliver  (11) | 117 |
| Catriona Wilcox  (9) | 118 |
| Jessica Ashby  (9) | 118 |
| Alex Rycroft  (9) | 119 |
| Bethany Bowles Moore  (10) | 119 |
| Joshua Kelly  (10) | 120 |
| Michael Creed  (9) | 120 |
| Peter Rycroft  (11) | 121 |
| Claire Bartlet  (11) | 121 |
| Chloe White  (10) | 122 |
| Jack Davey  (10) | 122 |

| | |
|---|---|
| Chris Arthurs  (9) | 123 |
| Lauren Griffin  (10) | 123 |
| Paige Amber Snuggs  (11) | 124 |
| Tom Barry  (10) | 124 |
| Connor McQueen  (9) & William Jacka  (10) | 125 |
| Chelsea Clapperton  (11) | 125 |
| Emily White  (10) | 126 |
| Bethan Wookey  (9) | 127 |
| Rhiannon Williams  (10) | 128 |
| Emma Chaning-Pearce  (11) | 129 |
| Lucy Speechley  (9) | 130 |
| Alice Fowler  (10) | 130 |
| Nicole Holden  (11) | 131 |
| Hollie Teagle  (9) | 131 |
| Chelsie Scarrott  (9) | 132 |
| Sally Keeley  (9) & Alistair Swift  (11) | 132 |
| Lily Taylor  (10) | 133 |
| Jodie Walker  (9) | 134 |
| Luke Davis  (11) | 134 |
| Elizabeth Coley  (10) | 135 |
| James Lucking  (10) | 135 |
| Amy McCauley  (10) | 136 |
| Charlotte Jeffs  (10) | 136 |
| Jessica Crockett  (10) | 137 |
| Brandon J Lawley  (10) | 137 |
| Suzanna Tyack  (11) | 138 |
| Demi Davies (9) | 138 |
| Lauren Baldwyn  (10) | 139 |
| Andrew Coyne  (9) | 139 |
| Ben Croft  (10) | 140 |
| Jack Oughton  (10) | 140 |
| George Wright  (10) | 141 |
| Ellie Marie Marshall  (9) | 141 |
| Sarah Thompson  (9) | 142 |
| Martin Bateman  (10) | 142 |
| Victoria Firth  (10) | 143 |
| Megan Jarvis  (9) | 143 |
| Rachel Firth  (10) | 144 |
| Liam Annakin  (11) | 144 |
| Sophie Halley  (9) | 145 |
| Sophie Marshall  (9) | 145 |
| Rosie Clark  (9) & Emily Sullivan  (10) | 146 |

James Stansbury  (9) — 146
Gaby Shakespeare  (11) — 147
Callum Gibson  (9) — 147
Kitty Teague  (11) — 148
Timothy Swatman Allen  (9) — 148
Keira-Mae Ladbrook  (11) — 149
Sam Dyer  (9) — 149

**St Lawrence CE Primary School, Lechlade**
Francesca Gardner  (11) — 150
Lawrence Gammond  (11) — 150
Charlotte Hall  (11) — 151
Jack Bestwick  (10) — 151
Benjamin Woodard  (10) — 152
Conrad Nuttall  (10) — 152
James Chase  (11) — 153
Stephen Watkins  (11) — 153
Lauren Bullock  (10) — 154
Isobel Stevens  (11) — 154
Ben Fisher  (10) — 155
Megan Fidler  (11) — 155
Matthew Knight  (11) — 156

**Uplands CP School**
Joshua Richter  (10) — 156
Jessica Vines  (9) — 157
Callum Webb — 158
Jennifer West  (9) — 158
Cameron Kyte  (11) — 159
Henry Cole  (10) — 159
McCoy Tinsey  (10) — 160
Jade Riches  (10) — 160
Ottilie Baker  (10) — 161
Ryan Thwaite  (11) — 162

**Watermoor Primary School**
Andrew Hartnell  (10) — 162
Megan Harding  (9) — 163
Sarah-Jane Greenhalgh  (10) — 163
Liam Tindal  (10) — 164

| | |
|---|---:|
| Kes Wilkie  (7) | 164 |
| Katie Sandell  (8) | 165 |
| Kieran Smith  (10) | 165 |
| Georgia Malone  (8) | 166 |
| Molly Simpson  (9) | 166 |
| Jonathan Sampson  (10) | 167 |
| Georgia Voce  (10) | 167 |
| Rachel Evans  (8) | 168 |
| Thomas Honey  (8) | 169 |
| Toby Riddle  (9) | 169 |
| Amy Gleed  (9) | 170 |
| Tezhara Esteves  (10) | 170 |

### Woodchester Endowed School

| | |
|---|---:|
| Molly O'Hara  (7) | 170 |
| Dorothy Scarborough  (9) | 171 |
| Iona Lautieri  (8) | 171 |
| Tom Fickling  (9) | 172 |
| Alexis Hall  (8) | 172 |
| Paul Sampson  (8) | 173 |
| Louise Mullen  (8) | 173 |
| Milan Alden  (8) | 173 |
| Freddie Waldon  (8) | 174 |
| Emily Radcliffe  (7) | 174 |
| Toby Redding  (9) | 174 |
| Isobel Lewis  (8) | 175 |
| Ben Jones  (7) | 175 |
| Tommy McInerney  (7) | 175 |
| Luke Daniels  (9) | 176 |
| Jack Lister  (7) | 176 |
| Sam Weller  (7) | 176 |
| Thomas Little  (8) | 177 |
| George Staniforth  (9) | 177 |
| George Drake  (8) | 178 |
| Isaac Fearnley  (7) | 178 |
| Molly Leech  (7) | 178 |

# The Poems

## The Pond

A pond,
Reeds pouring over water.
A flash of violet bounces softly,
As lily pads hover over opaque grey water.
Underneath the filthy rush, a frog
Sits upon a rock, vast eyes blazing.
Fish silently through magnificent gills
Before proceeding to a private area.
Beneath the bulging belly of the frog,
Its spawn wades in the water,
Small as the head of a needle.
Inside the jelly a tadpole forms,
A tiny explosion bursts the water,
An echo repeats from side to side.
Finally the tadpole is free.

**Georgia Miles (10)**
Beaudesert Park School

## Fireworks Night

Whirling, swirling, zooming, booming,
Shooting to the crisp night sky.
People meeting, greeting, eating,
Sipping wine, their spirits high.
Racing rockets to the moon,
Bonfires blazing, roaring, soaring.
Guy Fawkes burning, singeing, whinging
As his ash begins to fly.
Children running, shouting, laughing,
Neon crowns above their heads.
Eyes are wide and then they're tired,
It's time for them to go to bed.

**Rebecca Raby Smith (9)**
Beaudesert Park School

## Red

Red is for Mars, the great god of war,
He likes to fight more and more.

Red is for ants and their poisonous bite,
They sometimes lie in shade and sometimes in light.

Red is for the sunset across the sea,
When I swim small fish like to tickle me.

Red is for anger, blood and gore,
Ripped flesh, open cuts raw.

Red is for desert, barren and lifeless,
Nothing to eat or drink just plain wilderness.

Red is for the sun, amazing and gold,
Scorching hot, massive and bold.

Red is for radiation, pollution and burns,
Nuclear acid destroys all the ferns.

Red is for the heat, nothing better than it,
But if you get too hot expect to swear a bit.

**Thomas Hillman (9)**
**Beaudesert Park School**

## My Lolly

My belly bellows *bang!*
My lolly screeches *boom!*
It fires up to rebound throughout the room.
It strikes my lips with such force,
I can't resist its juicy claws.
The superiority, the essence, the slight scent of sour,
I'll have a hundred more within an hour!

**William Reid (9)**
**Beaudesert Park School**

## The King Of Beasts

As the king of beasts prowls upon the ground,
He waits for his feast, ready to pound.

He is the greatest hunter and never fails,
He loves it when his prey gets trapped in gales.

He has two cubs and loves them dearly,
He had a fight and lost them nearly.

They ran and ran and ran even more
And ate the leftovers of blood and gore.

He nearly lost his poor wife to wild boars,
But he fought them off with his powerful jaws.

He's now alone with his wife by his side,
Protecting his kingdom and his pride.

**Edward Rankin (9)**
**Beaudesert Park School**


## White

White is for love, gentle and calm
And nice, sticky, slippery hand balm.

White is for clouds, fluffy and wet
And all the pretty bracelets I sometimes get.

White is for burns on soft, pale skin,
Once I got one on my chubby chin.

White is for dreams, some scary, some nice,
Once in a dream I ate cold rice!

White is for anger when people shout
And teachers have to send children out.

White is for road signs saying slow down,
Sharks' teeth and my flowing nightgown.

**Alicia Muir (9)**
**Beaudesert Park School**

## White

White is for clouds which live in the sky,
But when the sun comes out say goodbye.

White is snow, cold and fun,
I wish it wouldn't melt in the sun.

White is for dreams, the BFG blew,
Once I cheerfully got stuck in glue.

White is for the froth on my coffee,
Slurped down with a bit of toffee!

White is for a bone going click, crack, crunch,
I found one in my fish for lunch.

White is paper on which I write to Santa Claus,
This year I got a puppy instead named, Mr Paws.

White is for the tooth I lost just yesterday,
I got a pound from the tooth fairy, hip hip hooray!

**Rosa Schofield (9)**
**Beaudesert Park School**


## At The End Of School
*(Inspired by 'At the End of School Assembly' by Simon Pitt)*

Billy Bubble popped out,
Calum Cook blazed out,
Fiona Fish got hauled out,
Gilbert Gunn zoomed out.

Henry Hunt shot out,
Melissa Mudd squelched out,
Rachel Rider galloped out,
Simon Silly sniggered out.

But Katy Key got locked in.

**Robert O'Malley (7)**
**Beaudesert Park School**

## Cats

Cats love to pounce and kill with their claws,
But they're not like big cats which make loud roars.

Cats are so cuddly and they make you laugh,
But the thing they hate most is having a bath.

Most cats are so fit, they practise gym,
My cat's lazy, but that's just him.

Cats are sometimes shy but it really isn't their fault
When they cross over the road and forget to halt.

Cats love to clean themselves, just like you,
I love my cat and he loves me too.

**Xan Somerset (9)**
**Beaudesert Park School**


## Gareth

Gareth, the goat loved going on a boat
With his friend, Sammie, the stoat.

They went on the river sailing away,
They did not want to go, they wanted to stay.

Sammie, the stoat had glistening fur,
He ate mice in summer and slept in winter.

Gareth, the goat climbed a very steep hill,
He stumbled and tumbled and couldn't keep still.

Gareth and Sammie were very good friends,
They lived happily together in a very small den.

**Freddie Waller (9)**
**Beaudesert Park School**

## Blue

Blue is for the sky,
I love to watch the birds as they pass by.

Blue is for the ocean, big and wide,
I swim with my friends, side by side.

Blue is for peace when it's lovely and calm,
But I hold on tight to my lucky charm.

Blue is for a big, playful dolphin,
Squirting water as thin as a pin.

Blue is for my socks that have a red patch
Which I have to wear in a football match.

Blue is for my big round eyes,
That everyone needs especially spies!

**Augusta Puckett (8)**
**Beaudesert Park School**


## Red

Red is for when people go out to fight
Right in the middle of the night.

Red is for a beautiful shining ruby,
Everyone wants one except my friend, Lucy.

Red is for some bright red lipstick
That Clemmie likes to slap on very thick.

Red is for Mars, the Roman god of war
Who never stops boasting and is thirsty for more.

Red is for danger, war and fears,
Lots of eyes are full of tears.

Red is for the scorching hot sun,
When it is sunny children have fun.

**Jessica Priest (8)**
**Beaudesert Park School**

## Chocolates

Mouth-watering truffles
In bright coloured wrappings.

Rich chocolate nougat
In shop windows napping.

Soft Belgium chocolates
That swallow up money.

Caramel hearts so
Tasty and runny.

Jaw breaking toffees
That silence us all.

White chocolate orange,
A segmented ball.

Rich nutty praline,
Such a delight.

Hazelnut clusters,
They're worth a fight.

All these chocolates
Are a dream.

So why do I
Get coffee cream?

**Katherine Dauncey (11)**
**Beaudesert Park School**


## Mouse - Haiku

A frightened dormouse
Nibbling rotten Cheddar cheese
Springs trap unaware.

**Freddie Wyld (9)**
**Beaudesert Park School**

## Blue

Blue is the colour of the deep wide ocean
Where big fish swim in slow motion.

Blue is the colour for calmness and peace,
Olympic colours in Ancient Greece.

Blue is the colour of the lovely sky
Where aeroplanes and birds fly.

Blue is the colour of the largest whale,
But when the hunters come it turns pale.

Blue is the colour of a bluebell wood,
I would pick all the flowers if only I could!

**Clemmie Melvin (8)**
**Beaudesert Park School**


## Red

Red is for the ruby, the powerful stone,
As stiff as a rock, as hard as a bone.

Red is for anger when people shout,
Teachers get mad and send you out.

Red means danger, death and fears,
Which makes people sad and full of tears.

Red is for autumn when the leaves turn red,
They blow through my window and land on my bed.

Red is for fighting and terrible wars,
Tigers in amphitheatres with enormous jaws.

Red is for evening when the sun goes down,
I walk up to bed in my dressing gown.

**Camilla Purves (8)**
**Beaudesert Park School**

## Winter
*(Based on 'Winter' by Judith Nicholl)*

Winter glided
Upon the green grass,
The frost slithered around,
Green turned to white and sparkly,
But with no sound.

Winter soared
Over the sea,
Dancing through the waves,
Icicles hung in the fresh air,
While winter shortened the days.

**Rachel Smith (11)**
**Beaudesert Park School**


## Winter
*(Based on 'Winter' by Judith Nicholl)*

Winter swept
Over the thinly iced lake,
Dressed the land in his coat,
The wisp and whimper of his presence
Causes him to laugh and gloat.

Winter leapt
Under the appearing moon
As the stars started to twinkle,
His diamond eyes turned everything to ice
While the last snow was sprinkled.

**Hermione Russell (10)**
**Beaudesert Park School**

## Winter
*(Based on 'Winter' by Judith Nicholl)*

Winter frost
Brings no sound to the forest,
Not a squeak, not even a bird.
Everywhere is silent,
Nothing can be heard.

Winter nipped
Like the early bird,
Someone needs to use their mind.
The trees are swaying, the wind is coming,
This dark prowler is unkind.

**Hector Millar (10)**
**Beaudesert Park School**


## Winter
*(Based on 'Winter' by Judith Nicholl)*

Winter tackled,
Chasing all life from the trees.
Crisp leaves that glitter and crunch,
Leaving everything dead in its path,
Eating every colour for lunch.

Winter glided
Over the ice,
Scurrying to escape are the forgotten fish.
Suffocating all in its path,
It is the killer's wish.

**Dominic Barrington (10)**
**Beaudesert Park School**

## A Beach

Sighing like an old man napping,
The sea shone brightly onto powder white sand.
A single palm
Stood silent,
Alone.
Hanging from it
Coconuts, brown and bristly like a father's chin.
Inside sweet juices seeping through the coarse flesh.

**Sebastian Chater-Davies (10)**
Beaudesert Park School


## The Wood

At first it is just a sea of trees,
Closer, I see a dead log like a chipped coffin.
Closer again, I see little holes in the log like lift shafts.
Even closer, I see lots of little bugs squirming.
Closer still, I see they are woodlice, some rolled up into little
                                                armoured balls.
Closer once more and they look like tiny tanks
Crashing into each other and flying all over the log.

**Alexander Ferrigno (10)**
Beaudesert Park School


## Black

Black is for death, destruction and doom,
All pouring out from one big tomb.

Black is for smoke that's created by heat,
For toast that is burnt and barbecued meat.

Black is for soot made from coal,
Found in mines down a deep, dark hole.

**Michael Young (9)**
Beaudesert Park School

## Ski Lift

The bubble moves marble like up the mountain,
Looking out, I see a girl emerge from
A little crooked chalet far below,
Her silver ski poles glitter in the sun.
With a wiggle of her hips she is off,
Leaving a trail in the crisp snow.
The clattering metal chair lift turns,
I glimpse her padded bottom
Gently lowering onto the sparkling seat
Squashing each gleaming ice crystal resting there.
My journey is over, as with a rattle
The bubble moves into the dark cavern.

**Laura Gordon Lennox (10)**
Beaudesert Park School


## The Nest

The trees are draped in their autumn layer,
Like a rock from the mountains the bark is all jagged,
Ancient, bristled and ragged.
Leaves are swaying swiftly,
Spinning to a lower branch where
Delicately perched is a cautiously balanced nest,
With twigs woven in different directions.
The blue speckled egg is silently still waiting to hatch.
Creaking the shell begins to crack,
A warm baby chick begins to emerge,
It is nestled in fluff,
Under the fluff there are two hungry eyes
Staring beadily,
Tracing my eyes.

**Isabella Boscawen (10)**
Beaudesert Park School

## Gentlemen Of Old

A giant man with a fine green coat,
Lots of long dangly green hair.
It sways in the wind,
Its feet dig into the ground
To the centre of the earth.
Standing tall.
It is stubborn and strong
But why won't people notice it?
Growing tall until people see
The beauty inside me.
A giant man with a fine green coat.

**Tom Dyson (10)**
**Beaudesert Park School**

## The Raging River

River rages as sharks swim
Through it.

Fins are just visible over the surface
Of the water.

River of green,
River of brown.

Raging but calm, ugly but beautiful,
Old but young . . .

River rages, sharks swimming swiftly.

**Freddie Clarke (9)**
**Beaudesert Park School**

## A Stray

I was left outside,
I was all alone
With no food or water,
Not even a bone.

I was not loved,
I was dumped in the street,
I tried to make friends
With the people I would meet.

Then I was found
By a man dressed in white,
I growled at him,
He'd given me a fright.

I was put on a lead
By this very same man,
Put in a box
And off in his van.

I was taken to a dogs' home
And put in a cage,
I was growled at by other dogs,
So I got in a rage.

Month after month
The people walked by,
Nobody wanted me
So I started to cry.

Then all of a sudden I'm picked by a man,
I run to his car as fast as I can,
I was loved in the day
And I slept well at night,
So even for me
Things can turn out alright.

**Katie Burridge (10)**
**Beaudesert Park School**

# Winter
*(Based on 'Winter' by Judith Nicholl)*

Winter crawled
Through the unsuspecting grass.
Silently came a raid,
Stealing the leaves from trees,
Freezing every blade.

Winter wailed
Through the glistening plains,
Covering everything he could.
He only ever smiles pulling on his frosty hood.

**Oliver Gardner (11)**
**Beaudesert Park School**

# Eagle

Eagle I saw you watching,
Piercing the sky
With heartless eyes
Like a desperate man with no place to go.
I wonder eagle what you watch,
Eagle I saw you watching.

Eagle I hear your cry
As a bullet flies towards you.
I see you fall from the sky,
Eagle I hear your cry.

Men laugh from the tracks below,
Eagle I wonder why they do it.
You are a creature as many others are,
A creature soon to be gone.

Oh eagle how I wish I could stop them.

**Holly Bartlett (11)**
**Bishops Cleeve Primary School**

## On The Football Pitch

On a gloomy horrible day
The match got under way
And then it got very boring
Until we started scoring.
When it came to half-time
Our manager said we'd played fine.

In the second-half
The opposition had a laugh.
Then the other team
Started to sparkle and gleam,
They had ace control
Which ended in a goal.

And it was when they thought they had won
The last goal went in, just one.
When the ref blew his whistle
Our manager sat on a thistle.
He jumped in the air
And lost his hair,
But who cares
We've won!

**Paul Lennon (11)**
**Bishops Cleeve Primary School**

## Seasons

Blossoms bloom in surprising spring.
Sun sparkles in super summer.
Leaves leave in awesome autumn.
Snow shimmers in wonderful winter.

**David McNair (11)**
**Bishops Cleeve Primary School**

## Be Strong

Sometimes we fade away,
But it can be better the next day.
We have to be strong, be strong.

Life is not always easy,
But we have to be bright and breezy.
Be strong, be strong.

We have got to be happy, be happy,
Otherwise we would be horrible and snappy.
Be strong, be strong.

Think of a happy thing,
And dance around and sing.
Be strong, be strong.

Just remember to be glad,
Not stroppy and sad.
And be strong.

**Charlotte White (10)**
**Bishops Cleeve Primary School**


## Seasons Of The World

In the spring the flowers start to bloom,
It starts to get warmer
And Easter will come soon.

In the summer it gets really hot,
You can play outside
And you can go to the park.

In the autumn the leaves start to fall,
The trees start to get bare
And it starts to get cool.

In the winter it starts to get cold,
You look forward to Christmas
And sledging in the snow.

**Yasmin Baig (10)**
**Bishops Cleeve Primary School**

## A Place In The Sun!

Off the plane, great! No rain!
All I can feel is the heat on my face - wow!
What a lovely place.
I step on to the coach and picture the view!
Look at the sky,
So lovely and blue.
We arrive at the beach,
People bathing by the sea
As I watch the waves splash briskly.
Palm trees swaying in the warm breeze.
I'm so pleased to be here.
When I lie on the golden sands my body stretches like a big hand.
Oh what a lovely day in this month of May.

**Gabriella Large (11)**
**Bishops Cleeve Primary School**


## Animals

This is a poem about animals
Because animals are wonderful things,
Some are furry and hairy,
Some are feathery and sing.

Some hiss and some roar,
Some fly and crawl,
Some are short and some tall,
In this poem we identify them all.

Dinosaurs and dodos died out long ago,
Most animals are alive and some are protected.
We do our best to keep them here,
After all we are descended and connected.

**Jade Musto (10)**
**Bishops Cleeve Primary School**

## Rumble In The Jungle!

The animals that live in the jungle
Can fly, slither and slide.
There's always a *rumble*.

Lions, leopards and lizards
Can appear here and there,
Not that different to some wizards.

There's an amazing, attractive animal
That swings from tree to tree,
Not that different to me.

The oval leaves dangle in the summery breeze,
The pine trees twist and bend,
Cracking just like my mum's knees!

The jungle is somewhere I've never seen,
I feel that the jungle is part of a dream,
A place I've never been.

The animals that live in the jungle
Can fly, slither and slide.
There's always a *rumble*.

**Grace Baker (11)**
**Bishops Cleeve Primary School**


## My Dog Barney

My dog Barney was black with brown,
He always said hello when we got back from town.
My dog Barney was as gentle as a mouse,
He spent most of the time outside the house.
My dog Barney, he wouldn't harm a fly,
If he couldn't sleep in Mum and Dad's room he would start to cry.
My dog Barney, he was my little baby,
Maybe he wouldn't have died if he wasn't so old, maybe, just maybe.

**Megan Sweeney (11)**
**Bishops Cleeve Primary School**

## My Family

Take my rich as can be dad, but Dad is dull, dopey and dumb,
Then there's my mum she's the clever one, ask her any sum.
And my grandad he's like a bull in a china shop,
But my nan keeps him on track, the mad manic mop.
My family's the best in the west
And that is no lie.
We rock this world
And have loads of fun, at the same time.

Then there are the cousins, they're really bouncy and brave,
My bogey brain lives in a cold creepy cave.
And my sister she's dark, dull and dreary,
But uncle isn't dumb he's wise, wonderful and weary.
Our family's the best in the west
And that is no lie.
We rock this world
And have loads of fun at the same time.

**Sophie Smith (11)**
**Bishops Cleeve Primary School**


## Footy Mad

There once was a boy who liked football,
He played in goal because he was tall
And that boy's name happened to be Paul.

He saved all the shots from inside the box,
But he would only admit it was his lucky socks
And boy did he take some nasty knocks.

So that tall, amazing, fandabidozzie goalie,
Saved a penalty and did a roly-poly
And that boy's name was Paul.

**David Pinco (10)**
**Bishops Cleeve Primary School**

## A Rainbow

Once I saw a rainbow way up high in the sky,
I had to go and follow it, it had caught my eye.
This end, that end, which end would it be?
I had to go and follow it and see what I could see.
I travelled far and wide to try to find your start,
I needed to know the secret of your beautiful coloured heart.
I hopped over red,
I skipped over yellow,
I jumped over pink and landed on green,
I slid down purple and stumbled on to orange
And bounced onto blue.
It was there I found the end of you.
Was there really a pot of gold?
I will not be the one who told.

**Emily Giles (10)**
**Bishops Cleeve Primary School**

## Bad To Good

Why can't I be good?
I know I should,
I do wish I could.
When I'm naughty and bad
I make my parents really sad,
It makes them feel as they're to blame,
I know it's me and I should retrain.

I will be good!
Because I know I should,
I will really try
To be a good guy.
I will not make my teachers cry!
I will think before I bubble,
Then there will be no more trouble . . .

**Jacob Wilkes (11)**
**Bishops Cleeve Primary School**

## I Am An Eagle

I am an eagle flying high,
Soaring across sapphire sky,
Over valleys, mountains and blue sea,
What a wonderful life for me.

I am an eagle ready to kill,
Here I swoop over the hill,
Little mouse in talons of steel,
You'll soon be a lovely meal.

I am an eagle ready to rest,
Looking for my cosy nest,
There it is on clifftop high,
My twiggy home near the sky.

I am an eagle ready to sleep,
Down below is dark and deep,
Tomorrow is another day,
For me to fly and hunt my prey.

**Gareth Jones (10)**
**Bishops Cleeve Primary School**


## Monster Land

In the land where monsters roam and prowl
There lived some creatures big and foul.
The sapla is eating a wompa plant
While the bookoo sucks the juices of an orange ant.
The zakalak sleeps in its watery den,
The giant ampidock feasts on some men.
Then the luckaply spots a weird creature,
Look it's the timbon with some very odd features.
Last the jazoo, wrinkled and frail
Eats the leftovers of a humongous snail.

**Amy Daglish (11)**
**Bishops Cleeve Primary School**

## Wrestlemania 21

Wrestlemania is nearly here,
I've been waiting for this for nearly a year,
But Brock Lesner wasn't here,
He broke his back for almost a year!

Before the bell rang John Cena had something to say,
He said he came from LA!
But John Cena came here for a reason,
To punch Booker T into the next season!

Eddie Guerrero had a match with Batista 'n' Jbl,
He used the five star frog splash and the match went very well,
But at the end he made the wrong move,
Then, the match didn't go very smooth.

Rey Mysterio 'n' Rvd had a match you had to see!
Rey Mysterio did the 619,
Which knocked out the opponent till half-past nine,
But that's not all, they won the belt,
And it was without any help!

**Jason Andrews (11)**
**Bishops Cleeve Primary School**


## My Cat

My favourite animal is my black and white cat
Who sleeps on my front door mat.
He gets in a mood
When I am late with his food
And when he's finished he lies on his back.
His white furry tummy looks very funny because he's full and fat.
When I am asleep in my bed he wakes me by lying on my head,
Then he miaows which makes me cross,
Then I shout at him telling him I am the boss.

**Joshua Barrett (10)**
**Bishops Cleeve Primary School**

# The Four Seasons

*Spring*
Spring is the time of year that
Everything comes to life,
Recovering from winter's
Frost and ice.
It's time for the new animals
To be born again and enjoy
Their new life.

*Summer*
Summer is the time of year
When we all come out to play
And the ice cream man drives
His van and we all shout hurrah.
Then the paddling pool comes out
And we invite our friends round.
We have so much fun I wish I could spend
All day in the sweltering hot sun.

*Autumn*
Autumn is the time of year
When it gets cold again
And the golden brown and red leaves fall off the trees
And the little squirrels collecting
Their food as fast as a cheetah to get as
Much as they can to last them
Through the winter.

*Winter*
Winter is the time of year
When the sky is grey and dull,
All the flowers die away and the trees
Are bare with no more life
But Christmas brings a smile to
Everybody's face and they sing with delight
And the children can't wait to
Open their presents and see what's
Inside and then a shower of snowflakes fall
From the sky and then the children go outside
To see their friends and build snowmen!

**Charlotte Holden (11)**
**Bishops Cleeve Primary School**

# Rugby

It was Gloucester Vs Stadfranceia
In the Heineken Cup.
Gloucester started a break play
And won all of the line outs when Jake Bower was lifted up.

Then in the changing rooms at half-time
The Stadfranceia players were very sad
Because their manager wasn't allowed to stand on the side line
But this made Gloucester very glad.

Then in the second-half
Stadfranceia were ready for a battle,
So before the game restarted the players were having a laugh
But when the Gloucester players came out the ground
Started to shake and rattle.

Then after the game,
Gloucester won 27-0,
Already the players had crowds giving them chants and fame
But for Stadfranceia losing in the Heineken Cup
Meant rather a large bill.

**Nathan Webb (10)**
**Bishops Cleeve Primary School**


# Another World

Glistening silver beads fly from the rippling sapphire sea,
As the pearl dolphin plunges into the new blue world,
Emerald seaweed and peach coral,
All disappearing just as quickly as they had emerged,
Schools of scarlet fish swim past,
As an agile body glides effortlessly around in the cool azure water
And then once again leaps back up into the sunlight.

**Bethan Reynolds (10)**
**Bishops Cleeve Primary School**

## Marooned On A Desert Island

As I look out across the sea
I wonder who will rescue me.
Will they see my SOS?
I very much hope the answer's yes.

While I'm here I must survive
And very much stay alive.
Food and water I must find
And build a shelter of some kind.
I need to feel safe and warm
And protected from a tropical storm.
Will I be alright at night and make
It through to morning light.

This island with its lush green vegetation
I know was made by God's creation.
The golden sand beneath my feet
Is soft and fine and full of heat.
The sun burns down throughout the day
And I can feel every ray.

I pray that I will soon be found
And very much homeward bound.

**Alastair Wade (11)**
**Bishops Cleeve Primary School**


## Sunrise

Pink fluffy clouds drifting dreamily,
A chorus of birds singing and talking,
The wetness of the dew on blades of grass,
A chilly breeze slowly being wiped away by the sun's warm rays,
Air that is fresh and clear.
The sound of cows going to be milked,
The smell of earth beneath my feet.

A golden glow growing in the east.

**Emily Stone (10)**
**Bishops Cleeve Primary School**

## Seasons

It's almost springtime, flowers are showing,
We look to how the garden's growing,
It's been a long winter but now we're knowing
Things are starting to come to life.
After this we look forward to summer,
Hopefully that will be a hummer.
It's then looking to autumn when trees turn red,
The gardens and plants look good in their beds,
It's then we are preparing for frost and cold,
We should prepare to be very bold.

**George Curr (10)**
**Bishops Cleeve Primary School**

## My Jumper

This weekend I went to my gran's to play
Because it was my tenth birthday.
I knew my gran wouldn't buy me jeans because I was getting plumper,
As I burst through the door my excitement ended because on the
Kitchen table was a woolly jumper.
As I collapsed on the floor from the fashion disaster
I hit my head on the door and needed a plaster.
When I woke up later my gran stood above me,
My head was spinning and I couldn't see,
Unfortunately I could still see the jumper, it was fluffy and pink
And I just about made it to the sink,
When I got home my mum made me put it on,
But all I wanted was for it to be *gone*.
I'm dreading the thought of my 11th birthday,
Next year I'm not visiting Gran I'm going to stay at home to play.

**Megan Frost (10)**
**Bishops Cleeve Primary School**

## Monday To Friday!

It was Monday morning and I was late,
Didn't get out of bed till half-past eight.

I couldn't find my sock and I couldn't find my shoe,
I needed a bath and I didn't know what to do.

I sat in the bath at 8.51, I know that I was gonna get very done,
I got to school at 9.08, the whistle had gone and I was very late.

Mrs White was very mad, she shouted at me which made me sad,
After that I was very good, got up on time just like I should.

Friday came and I'd been nice and neat,
Guess what I got?

*Yeah*, star of the week!

**Jack Watts (10)**
**Bishops Cleeve Primary School**


## Colours

Yellow is the colour of the bright shining sun,
Yellow is the colour of the golden sand,
Yellow is the colour of a sour lemon,
Yellow is a tulip blowing in the breeze,
Yellow is the colour of butter spreading lightly,
Yellow is the buttercups growing in the field.

Pink is a blush when you feel silly,
Bubblegum stuck to your teeth,
Soft fluffy slippers,
Freshly scrubbed fingers,
Pink like a mouse underneath.

Red is bright red lipstick,
Roses standing still in the field,
Red is a red nose,
Red is juicy tomatoes,
Red is a pencil crayon.

**Daisy Green (10)**
**Bishops Cleeve Primary School**

## I Telephoned The School One Day And Someone Said . . .

'Matthew's got the measles,
Megan's got the mumps,
Amy says her hair's on fire
And Ben's come out in lumps.

Hannah broke her arm
Jumping on the bed,
Charlotte's at home
With a bandage on her head.

Anna feels sick,
Chris does too,
Toby has a tummy ache
And needs the loo.

Everyone is ill today,
Everyone in sight,
Please ring back tomorrow
Because the head has just gone white.'

**Jessica Belcher (10)**
**Bishops Cleeve Primary School**


## Saturday

I crawl out of bed
Knowing what lies ahead.
I get washed and dressed,
Then go for breakfast,
I have cereals and toast,
The meal I love the most.
I get my coat and shoes,
Then Mum gives me some news,
'Lee there's no school today,
Have you forgotten, it's Saturday!'

**Lee Parry (10)**
**Bishops Cleeve Primary School**

## The Old Bridge

The old bridge was an old creaky bridge,
Never touched by a foot, never disturbed.
Only a frog or two jumped on it from the
Ice-cold stream, that ran below.

It stood rotting, hoping that
Soon it would be touched.
One day there came a slight
*Tap, tap* of footsteps.

The old bridge was slowly
Cracking, as the footsteps came
Closer, until *crash*
The old bridge gave away.

The old bridge was an old creaky bridge,
Never touched by a foot, never disturbed.
Only a frog or two jumped on it from the
Ice-cold stream, that ran below.

**Ben Carson (10)**
**Bishops Cleeve Primary School**


## Senses

I'm in the country, I can hear
The sound of the train coming nearer and nearer.

I'm on the beach, I can see
The waves crashing up against me.

I'm in the garden, I can taste
The sweet taste of ice cream trickling down my face.

I'm in the fairground, I can
Smell the hot dogs and onions done very well.

I'm on the farm, I can feel
Soft, squidgy mud against my heel.

**Lauren Dix (11)**
**Bishops Cleeve Primary School**

## Wartime

Families were parted
When World War II started.
They took gas masks in cases
And very sad faces.

They went on a train
And were caused lots of pain.
Few were happy,
Many were sad.

Hundreds went back,
Some stayed,
A few live now to tell us of those days.

**Dominic Evans (10)**
Bishops Cleeve Primary School

## Under A Fairy's Spell

Never go a-hunting
In the trees of the Swigswag Wood,
For a tribe of troublesome fairies
Dwell in a lonesome rood.
'Twas a time in the middle age
When peasants first feared their rage,
Hunters never knew when they were unsafe
While a-hunting in the Swigswag Wood,
But the sound of their muskets enraged the fairies
And they scuttled from their woeful den.
The hunters tried their best to frighten the creatures,
But after a struggle, gave in to their evil fiends.
They disappeared without a trace,
So never go a-hunting
In the trees of the Swigswag Wood.

**Roxanne Blake (11)**
Bishops Cleeve Primary School

## The Thing

The thing is gigantic and hairy,
Absolutely humongous and scary.
It will give you a fright
In the dark, gloomy night,
With a big bash and boom!
The loud clanking of doom!

As it climbed up the stairs
I heard the rustle of its hairs,
I gave a loud shriek,
My door opened with a creak,
I hid under the sheet
And my heart missed a beat.

It jumped on my bed
And searched for my head,
As it sniffled around
My heart began to pound.
It was heavy like a log
And then I realised . . .
The thing was my dog!

**Penny Sparrow (10)**
**Bishops Cleeve Primary School**


## Places

Towns and cities, mountains and hills,
Rivers, villages and old windmills,
Countryside, pubs and even a skate park,
McDonald's and restaurants that open at dark,
A post office, pedestrians, even some signs,
Tesco's, wardens and double yellow lines,
Bus stops, markets and a public phone,
But my favourite of all has got to be my home!

**Gareth Lee (10)**
**Bishops Cleeve Primary School**

## Animals

Animals that jump, animals that bite,
Some animals can give you a fright.
Monkeys are so cheeky,
Sometimes they can be squeaky.
What are you going to do
When a lion roars at you?
Elephants are so fat
That they could squash you flat.
When it's quarter past eight
Kangaroos come out to date.
When you kill a lizard
There are normally blizzards.
Some animals are harmless
And some are charmless.
Animals are sometimes dodgy
And can be podgy.
This is the end of my poem
And I must be going.

**Neil Bell (10)**
**Bishops Cleeve Primary School**


## The Fireman

My hero is the fireman
Who works and trains each day.
This man can do more than anyone can
To keep us out of harms way.

The engine red and bright
Can be seen by day and night.
You can see the engine from a mile or two,
The lights of which are bright and blue.

Many lives are saved each day
Because of the men who are so brave,
The engine's racing, bells ringing,
Lives saved, people singing.

**Sam Mitchell (11)**
**Bishops Cleeve Primary School**

# Skipping Ropes

There once was a girl called Samantha Pope
And she always played on her skipping rope,
However it broke,
Poor Samantha Pope,
It broke,
The skipping rope.

Next she took down the washing line,
To skip with it was fine,
However it broke,
Poor Samantha Pope,
It broke,
The line she used as a rope.

Next she took the dog's lead,
She promised him an extra feed,
However it broke,
Poor Samantha Pope,
It broke,
The lead she used as a rope.

Next she took Dad's computer cable,
She found it under his office table,
However it broke,
Poor Samantha Pope,
It broke,
The cable she used as a rope.

Next she couldn't find anything to use,
There was nothing left for her to choose,
However they had all broke,
It wasn't funny, it was no joke,
There is nothing left for Samantha Pope,
What will she use for a skipping rope?

**Sara Gazzal (10)**
**Bishops Cleeve Primary School**

## The Four Seasons

Winter is cold
And the trees are bald.
The ground is white and covered in snow,
Father Christmas says, 'Ho, ho.'

Snowdrops, crocuses, all in a row,
Followed by daffodils who have come to say 'Hello'.
The brown prickly hedgehog wakes up from his sleep,
Pokes his nose out to take a peep.

Paddling pool in the garden,
No need for a cardigan,
Don't forget to have a lolly,
Everybody's warm and jolly.

Autumn leaves are falling down,
Red, orange, gold and brown.
The winds are blowing
And the river's overflowing.

**Emily Beuzelin (10)**
**Bishops Cleeve Primary School**


## My Life

I am a ten year old girl
And I control my own mind,
I twirl and whirl
And I can sometimes be kind.

I have a brother, a sister and a dog I love
And as far as I know
They were sent from above.

My mum and my dad
They can sometimes be mean
And if netball is involved
I am there and I am keen.

So there you have it,
There is my life.

**Francesca Baillie (10)**
**Bishops Cleeve Primary School**

## Pancake Pop

Hear it crackle, hear it pop,
Pour on the syrup drop by drop.
Gobble it up while nice and hot,
Before you know it you've ate the lot.

My sister is crying, she only ate one,
I ate six and my brother had a ton.
We need some more we cry at Mum,
It's once a year, let's have some fun!

**Chloe Webb (11)**
**Bishops Cleeve Primary School**

## Night

Night is like a weird robber in my bedroom
Where the evil devil ghosts go
In my very own bedroom.

**Harry Notman (9)**
**Bledington Primary School**

## The Waterfall

Has surged water for many years,
It is azure, generous and majestic,
As muscular as a bull's charge,
As beautiful as a silver scaled fish,
It makes me feel so glad that I was there to capture this moment,
I feel so alive now I have seen the water of life,
The waterfall,
It reminds me of how life goes on.

**Lee Coles (11)**
**Bledington Primary School**

## The Almighty Moon

The almighty moon
Hanging in the starlit sky,
Enormous, stunning, dazzling,
Like an artist never failing to amaze.
As blinding as the sun on a summer's day,
It makes me feel tiny
Like a helpless ant.
The almighty moon,
It reminds us just how important life is.

**Ben Pocock (10)**
**Bledington Primary School**


## The Cave

Down in the cave where nobody goes
You'll find a skeleton in a pile of bones,
Rattle, crack, shiver
Like the door to Hell,
Like a hole in the skull,
It makes you feel dead but are you still alive?
The cave,
You'll never know if you'll ever come out,
Will you ever come out before the end of your life?

**Eira Walling (11)**
**Bledington Primary School**

## The Forest

The forest in the middle of the world,
The forest that was formed by gold,
The forest gleaming in the night,
The forest that was found by light.

The forest with green hanging vines,
The forest with webs so fine,
The forest that was cold and bright,
The forest with land, only black and white.

The forest that was never there,
The forest is only my dream.

**Toby Taylor (9)**
**Bledington Primary School**


## The Cave

The cave,
Discovered 100 years ago,
Creepy, mysterious, scientific,
It's as creepy as a haunted house,
It's as dark as midnight,
I feel as if I am being watched,
I feel cold, as cold as ice,
The cave,
It reminds me of a dead dinosaur's jaw!

**Hayley Jarvis (10)**
**Bledington Primary School**

## The Ancient Jungle

The ancient jungle,
Used by thousands of stranded people,
Spooky, mysterious, dark,
Trees like mountains,
Bushes as big as boulders,
It makes me feel scared,
Like an elephant crawled on by a mouse,
The ancient jungle
Reminds us of sadness.

**Edina Morris (9)**
**Bledington Primary School**


## The Old Bedroom

The old bedroom has creaky floorboards,
It hasn't been used since the ancient Egyptians,
It is creepy, dark and gloomy,
As dark as the pitch-black night sky.
As gloomy as a haunted house that a witch could live in,
It makes me feel frightened,
As frightened as a little mouse being killed by a cat.
The old bedroom reminds me of death,
The old room makes me think of my rabbit
Screeching because it was being killed.

**Toni Wilton (9)**
**Bledington Primary School**

## Night-Time

Night is like a drift of cold air,
Where dreams come alive,
In my bedroom.

Night is like a clever owl,
Where bats fly,
In creepy land.

Night is like a bell ringing,
Where wind blows,
In the church.

**Becky Pearson (8)**
Bledington Primary School


## The Starry Night

*(Inspired by 'Silver' by Walter De La Mare)*

Twinkling, twirling, shooting stars go by,
They look like they're watching all with an eye.
Ebony black falls on a shadowy tree,
What a still, silent life the stars can see.
Owls are hooting from a height,
Foxes are not moving at all with fright.
Silver fishes are still in a gentle flowing stream,
Everything seems to be hiding not dared to be seen.
Then the dazzling sun comes in sight,
Morning is coming, the colours are getting bright.

**Ellen Lockstone (9)**
Cam Hopton CE Primary School

## The Starry Night
*(Inspired by 'Silver' by Walter De La Mare)*

Twinkling, twirling, shooting stars
Bright stars float around Mars
Big-eyed frogs lay still on the lily pad
The dull stars are very gloomy
The midnight sky is very loomy
The fish in the stream swim side to side
Jupiter is trying to hide
The big snowy owl tried hooting
The stars one by one are shooting
The cockerel wakes remembering his duty.

**Elizabeth Grimshaw (8)**
**Cam Hopton CE Primary School**


## The Starry Night
*(Inspired by 'Silver' by Walter De La Mare)*

On a starry night,
When the moon was bright
And the daffodils like stars are blooming,
The midnight-black sky is looming.
Down in the garden the mice scuttle round,
The hedgehogs and badgers start to bound,
The sly ginger foxes start to prowl,
The dark grey wolves begin to howl.
The sun starts to come in sight,
Morning is coming, it brings us light.

**Alice Clarke (9)**
**Cam Hopton CE Primary School**

## The Starry Night
*(Inspired by 'Silver' by Walter De La Mare)*

Twinkling, twirling stars are shooting
Golden-eyed owls are gently hooting
Flowers gold like the sun
The moon is still as round as a bun
The golden shine still comes through
See the snow-white dove as he flew
Soon the daffodil comes golden too
Before they wake to see you.

**Megan Hambling (8)**
**Cam Hopton CE Primary School**


## The Starry Night
*(Inspired by 'Silver' by Walter De La Mare)*

Ebony, eerie night
A lair is nearby with a fright,
It's by the polar bear,
With silver eyes and golden fur,
A ginger cat with a beautiful purr
Has moonlit eyes and gruesome claws
Creeping along with its fearsome paws,
Creepy things flying all over the place
Shooting stars have run the race.

**Zoe Latuszka (9)**
**Cam Hopton CE Primary School**

## The Starry Night
*(Inspired by 'Silver' by Walter De La Mare)*

Twinkling, twitching, shooting stars go past,
Tiny little mice are scuttling very fast.
Midnight black makes the trees look doomed,
One of the trees almost loomed.
Foxes hunt for food at night,
Under stars that shine very bright.
Lots of birds are tweeting loudly,
The ginger cat prances proudly.

**Cara Froggatt (9)**
**Cam Hopton CE Primary School**


## Starry Night
*(Inspired by 'Silver' by Walter De La Mare)*

When I look out of my bedroom
Stars are twinkling through the mist
People are visiting their family and friends
Birds are flying through the fog
And when I look down I see foxes
And when I look in the trees
Owls are hooting through the leaves.

**Kane Loveridge (9)**
**Cam Hopton CE Primary School**


## Springtime

I see green fields from afar
It sounds like a sheep being sheared
It tastes like snow when snowdrops are blooming
It smells of silage just being made
It feels warm, you could sunbathe
It reminds me of when I was born.

**Lucy Topham (8)**
**Deerhurst & Apperley CE Primary School**

## Summer

Summer is like the best day of your life
It wakes you up every morning because the colours have come out
Summer tastes like hot fire
Summer smells like colourful flowers growing in the atmosphere
Summer heat never goes away
Summer reminds you of water
Summer makes you feel full of energy.

**Katie Atkinson (11)**
**Deerhurst & Apperley CE Primary School**


## Sadness

Sadness is grey and sadness is blue,
Sadness is horrible but very true.
Sadness is grey, there can't be any play,
Sadness is grey, you have to say.

Sadness tastes like sour cream,
You know you must be in a bad dream
Sadness is like an orchestra too tired to play
You want to escape to another day.

Sadness smells like blueberry pie past its sell-by date
Oh, sadness is a thing I hate
Sadness feels like wearing no coat
In a storm that feels its grasping your throat.

Sadness looks like a blue blanket
Trapping every happy moment
Sadness reminds me of being on a mountain,
Alone.

**Hannah Street (9)**
**Deerhurst & Apperley CE Primary School**

## Summer

Summer is bright like a light
Summer is not dark live a cave
Summer tastes like a drop of the sun
Summer looks like strawberries floating in the air
Summer feels like you're on holiday on the beach eating ice cream
Summer sounds like waves crashing into the bay
Summer tastes like golden syrup in lemon tea
Summer reminds me of all my old friends playing in the grass,
But they have left for secondary school
Summer also reminds me of my cat Maisie
Playing in the grass, catching mice.

**Hannah Stephens (10)**
**Deerhurst & Apperley CE Primary School**

## Spring

In the sunny spring
I can hear the bells ring
I feel so joyful
But it is so beautiful
Some people are happy
Some plants are snappy
One of the plants are the king
All the others sing
I can see some light
But I can see a dreadful sight
I love the smell
But some people yell
All the flowers sleep
By the hum of the sheep.

**Isabella Bourne (10)**
**Deerhurst & Apperley CE Primary School**

## Fear

Fear is dark grey like a spiky rubber ball
As you try to grab it, the fear comes out to tease you
It smells like a mouldy tree in a damp, rotten forest
It sounds like a very low whistle that you can't control or ignore
It looks like loads of jagged sparks flashing across your eyes
Fear reminds me of explosions, storms and panic.

**Roshin Ono (9)**
**Deerhurst & Apperley CE Primary School**


## Anger

Anger is like red-hot embers
Anger tastes like a sour grapefruit
Anger sounds like my mum screaming
Anger reminds me of red and black
Anger feels like hands slapping me
Anger glares red like ambulance lights
Anger looks like a charging bull
Anger is like a broken back
Anger!

**Luke Ridal (9)**
**Deerhurst & Apperley CE Primary School**


## Darkness

Darkness is a creeping demon,
Darkness is the shadow of night,
You cannot touch it,
You cannot smell it,
You cannot hear it,
It tastes like fresh morning air,
It's like a horrible monster closing in on you
Every night.

**Charlie Wiseman (10)**
**Deerhurst & Apperley CE Primary School**

## Springtime

Springtime is somewhere where I watch the creatures grow
They eat the green, green grass where flowers and plants grow
It makes me smile when I see the world get happier and happier
It feels like the water trickling so peacefully down my back
It sounds like the birds singing so peacefully and happily
It tastes like some melons so ripe and sweet
It smells of the flowers that bring happiness to me
I wish springtime would never go, but when it does I'll never forget.

**Amie Booth (9)**
**Deerhurst & Apperley CE Primary School**


## Darkness

Darkness is the nocturnal demon,
Darkness is the shadow of day,
Its aroma is filthy and bitter like the loneliest corner in Hell,
You cannot hear it,
You cannot see it,
You cannot touch it,
Heed the warning of the sunset,
For darkness is coming
You cannot escape it.

**Robert Tattersall (11)**
**Deerhurst & Apperley CE Primary School**


## Darkness

When darkness appears
It feels like a ghost is following me around all night.
When I look out the window and all I can see is blackness.
Suddenly the heating is turned off
It smells like petrol has been spilled all over the floor.

**Lillie Stacey (7)**
**Deerhurst & Apperley CE Primary School**

## Mountain River

A river flowing down the mountain
And fish scooting down the river hurrying along.

Mountains as high as the sky
Makes the wind sing a song.

Grass blowing and flowers swaying next to the river's path
And people fishing in the river drinking from a flask.

It makes me feel relaxed, happy and comfortable
And it makes me happy to watch people climbing up the
                                            mountain's wall.

I can hear the wind blowing and birds tweeting and never stop
It makes me feel so happy to be by the river's plot.

**Rebecca Smith (10)**
**Ellwood Community Primary School**


## Jaguar

Jungle sounds, monkeys howling,
Snakes hissing
Bushes rustling all around
A jaguar watching from up above
Twigs snapping from down below.

The dampness of the ground
I'm being followed, watched.

Spiders making their webs,
Snakes sliding round my feet,
Eyes staring.

The jaguar is close
It's hunting me down.

**Rhiannon Thomas (11)**
**Ellwood Community Primary School**

## Bonfire Night!

Bright fireworks exploding in the sky, while men lazily load the holders.
Glowing torches shine through the black night,
far back from burning furniture flying off the bonfire.
People stand back hot from the heat,
while others quite cold come close.
Children who are excited jump up and down,
but parents stop them scared they will die.
Crowds cheering and talking about the screaming fireworks overhead
not to mention the loud bonfire crack.
Bright fireworks exploding in the sky, while men lazily load the holders.

**Amy Wallace (10)**
**Ellwood Community Primary School**


## The Small Boy

Deep, deep down in the alley,
A boy, young and scraggy,
Only about three foot five
Begging for his life.

Then along came a woman,
To ask what was the matter,
But when she walked over,
He moved backward frantically and along came a clatter.

And she said in a quiet voice . . .
'Don't worry come on, come home with me!'
Deep, deep down in the alley there was a boy young and scraggy,
But where is he now?

**Lotti Davies (11)**
**Ellwood Community Primary School**

## My Horse

I have a horse called Lucky,
She's very, very mucky.

When I touch her head,
She likes to go to bed.

When I feel her muddy fur,
She says to me, 'Bur.'

I feed her raw carrots,
I buy them from ferrets.

When I walk away,
She likes to go and play.

If I listen carefully,
I hear my horse, Lucky.

**Bethan Harper (10)**
**Ellwood Community Primary School**


## Soldier

Dark black bullets whizzing here and there,
People with nervousness and fear,
Injured people's bodies covered in blood.

I feel torture inside and out,
Great pain comes before me, but
Hopefulness is still about.

Generals calling orders,
People screaming and dying,
Crying men praying for peace.

**Amy Albury (10)**
**Ellwood Community Primary School**

## Cleopatra

I'm Queen Cleopatra, I love watching the orangy, sandy view
With the great pyramid beyond it
My gold and silver treasures, are more than just special
I remember when I first sat on my throne
Most of all I love my necklace made of gold
I feel my heavy gold and silver jewellery
It's really dragging me down
My clothes so silky on my skin
A comfortable head-dress on my head
So pretty and as light as gin
I can hear my workers scream for the whip that hits them
I hear my father shouting at the slaves
To put this on that and that on this.

**Georgina Jury (10)**
**Ellwood Community Primary School**


## Michael Owen

This is a poem,
About Michael Owen
He scores lots of goals
And wears golden soles.

He moved to Madrid
Because he only got paid a quid
He plays for England
And scored against Finland.

Before a match he's very tense
He volleyed right over and hit the fence
But when he's with Downing
You always see them frowning.

**Jack Smith (11)**
**Ellwood Community Primary School**

## My Football Poem

I'm Ian Wright
I'll try with all my might
To save every shot
If I save a shot, it's a jackpot
For me and my team.

They're taking a penalty
Oh what a great save!
I kick the ball, my team collect it
Then they take a shot
And guess what!
We've scored
Now it's 1-0 to my team.

We're back on
And they take another shot
I've saved it!
I kicked it
Oops, it went out of play
We're doing really well, me and my team.

I'm Ian Wright
I'll try with all my might
To save every shot.

**Ryan Hollis (10)**
**Ellwood Community Primary School**


## Anger

It sounds like the shout of The Hulk
The colour blood-red
It tastes like bitter onion
It smells like dried sweat
All screwed up and dangerous
It feels like you want to wreck everything
It reminds me of the grey Hulk.

**Joseph Stevenson-Challice (9)**
**Ellwood Community Primary School**

## Football Poem

What can you see?
The curious crowd cheering you on
With their shirts, scarves and hats.
The black and white leather ball in the middle of the pitch.

What can you feel?
You feel scared just in case you let in a goal
You're full of sweat from the tension.

What can you hear?
You can hear the whistle as you take the kick-off
You can hear the crowd cheering your name.

**Kieran Williams (10)**
**Ellwood Community Primary School**


## My War Poem

I can see people being killed
Guns being shot and big bombs
Exploding knives being thrown
I can see aeroplanes flying.

I feel pain growing inside me
And sadness flowing around me
And anger in my fists.

I can hear people screaming for help
Shouting for the pain to stop
I can hear planes crashing and bashing
I can hear guns being shot.

**Thomas Gwilliam (10)**
**Ellwood Community Primary School**

## Steven Gerrard

You can see players cheering on their terrific teams
You can see hats and scarves,
The colossal crowd showing their shirts
You can see the crazy coach shouting at everyone.

You can feel the pressure
When you take a penalty
You can feel sweat dripping off your body
You can feel happy when you score a golden goal for your team.

You can hear the crammed crowd crying your name
You can hear the referee blowing his beloved whistle
You can hear yourself puffing and panting.

**Conor Burris (9)**
**Ellwood Community Primary School**


## Ronaldo

When you walk you plainly see,
You are know better than ABC.
Thousands of people all around,
For you and your team making a stand.

When you walk out you feel like jelly
And there are butterflies in your belly.
You are the best, there is nothing to fear.

You hear the booing and the cheers
Hear the crowd
Hear your name
It is a lovely sound.

**Damian Farr (11)**
**Ellwood Community Primary School**

## Happiness

It sounds like a lovely cheer from the football hitting the net
It is a cool pink like a beautiful flower
It tastes like a piece of chocolate cake
It smells like my orange shampoo
It looks like a baby laughing
It's like a little kiss on your cheek
It is like a wonderful smile from my mum.

**James Hawkins (8)**
Ellwood Community Primary School


## Anger

Anger is like five million people shouting in a rugby stadium
It is like a bright white light that blinds you
It is like a plate full of cabbage
It is like rotting apples
It is like a broken door that I have punched
It is like drowning in a swimming pool
It is like my teacher telling me to do something I do not want to do.

**Jack Neale (9)**
Ellwood Community Primary School


## Happiness

It sounds like laughing
It's the colour of light pink
It tastes sour and sugary
It smells like cherries and strawberries
It looks like hugging and playing
It feels gentle and soft
It reminds me of my family hugging me.

**Sophie Cotterell (9)**
Ellwood Community Primary School

## Anger

Anger sounds like a boom of a drum inside my head
Anger is the colour of a red-hot fire
Anger tastes like a numbness in my mouth
Anger smells like sweat against my face
Anger looks like a dark cave
Anger feels like my brain is going to explode
Anger reminds me of when my brother is laughing at me.

**Charlotte Wells (10)**
**Ellwood Community Primary School**


## Happiness

It sounds like a cheerful laugh inside
It's bright yellow like the sun
It tastes like chocolate sponge that melts in my mouth
It smells like the breeze that's been sprayed
It looks like a real fun friend that can't see
It feels like a real soft polar bear hugging me
It reminds me of a friend that moved away
And she was a really funny friend.

**Emily Jones (9)**
**Ellwood Community Primary School**


## Happiness

It sounds like a purring kitten
Its colour is pink like strawberries in a fruit bowl
It looks like a flower gleaming
It tastes like a big piece of chocolate cake with cream
It smells like all different kinds of flowers
It looks like a flower gleaming in the sunshine
It feels like a fluffy white carpet
It reminds me of a hug from my mum.

**Bridie Downey (9)**
**Ellwood Community Primary School**

## Anger

Anger sounds like another winning goal from the other team
It is dark red like exploding tomatoes
It tastes like a bitter chocolate bar
It smells like steam from a saucepan
It looks like a black cloud in the sky
It feels like a fist of hate
It reminds me of when Wales beat England.

**Thomas Rushton (8)**
Ellwood Community Primary School


## Anger

Anger is like booming rockets
Anger is like a red fire burning
Anger is like a horrible sandwich
Anger smells like a soggy fire
Anger looks like mouldy bananas
Anger feels like rats' tails
Anger reminds me of me and my sister fighting.

**Zoe Pendrey (10)**
Ellwood Community Primary School


## Anger

It sounds like the war
It's bright red like blood
It tastes bitter like salt
It smells like sweat when you wipe it off your forehead
It looks like a rampaging bull
It feels like you're about to explode
It reminds me of World War 1.

**Thomas Brown (9)**
Ellwood Community Primary School

## Worry

Worry sounds like thumping and shouting
Worry is the colour of black like the dark night
Worry tastes dry and bubbly like small bubbles
Worry smells like sweat dripping down my face
Worry looks like fire smoking at night
Worry feels like a bubbly feeling in your hand
Worry reminds me of when my mum was sick.

**Grace Paddock (9)**
Ellwood Community Primary School

## Anger

Anger sounds like my sister shouting
Its colour is like red roses
It tastes like smelly cheese
It smells like rotten apples
It looks like hungry sharks
It feels like I want to smash something
It reminds me of fighting with my brother.

**Ben Morse (10)**
Ellwood Community Primary School

## Anger

Anger sounds like a witch laughing
Anger is the colour of dark red like lava from a volcano
Anger tastes like lettuce in my mouth
It smells like gone-off cream
It looks like a dragon running at me
It feels like hairspray up my nose
It reminds me of not staying on the beam in gym class.

**Fiona Bott (9)**
Ellwood Community Primary School

## Happiness

Happiness sounds like twittering birds in the breeze
It is a pretty peach colour in a fruit bowl
It tastes like sweet chocolate melting
It smells like the beautiful morning springtime
It looks like my mum's beautiful smile
It feels like a big warm hug off my mum
It reminds me of all my teachers, friends and family being there for me.

**Rachel Stephenson (9)**
Ellwood Community Primary School

## Love

It sounds like a little voice calling me
The colour is a soft cream like a bed
It tastes like sweet milk
And it smells like a soft aroma of lavender
Love looks like a swirling white cloud
And it feels like a soft blanket
And it feels like a hug off my mum and dad.

**Tori Maddock (8)**
Ellwood Community Primary School

## Hunger

Hunger sounds like sizzling, popping sausages in a pan
Hunger is the colour of brown stains in a pot
Hunger tastes like pizza cooked by my mum
Hunger smells like food floating through the air
Hunger looks like a pot and oven monster
Hunger makes me feel like I could float through the air
It reminds me of my mum cooking.

**Jack Akers (10)**
Ellwood Community Primary School

## Anger!

Anger sounds like the anger of soldiers in Word War II
The colours are grey and yellow of fire
It tastes of *nasty* war over Germany
It smells dirty
It looks *bloody*
It feels sad and miserable
It reminds me of *anger!*

**Jack Edmunds (10)**
**Ellwood Community Primary School**


## Anger

It sounds like a drum pounding in my head
Its colours are grey and sludgy-black like a wizard's long cloak
It tastes like green mushy peas on my plate
It smells like leaking gas or a horrible skunk
It looks like an underwater dragon or an ogre
It feels rough and hairy
It reminds me of a tornado hitting me in the face.

**Liam Jones (9)**
**Ellwood Community Primary School**


## In The War

War means blood and anger
Pain, bombs crashing in the dark night.

Aeroplanes overhead
Only four rounds left
What's going to happen?
*Bang!*
You have no time to wait.

**Sam Hatton (11)**
**Ellwood Community Primary School**

## Forest

The trees are swaying hard in the forest like they will never stop
You can see the water lilies bobbing up and down in the slimy pond
The little mites are trying to go through them, but they cannot go
There are snowdrops everywhere in the forest
Lots of grass and trees
Lots of lovely things.

I am always looking forward to going to the forest to see the
                                                          fish swimming
The lovely song of the birds singing and those spitting things
I just do not understand why they had to put those horrible
                                                    spitting llamas in the field
Now I can hear the trees creaking and squeaking
And streams flowing like they will never stop
Big mountains high, small, medium and large
Like they will never stop growing again.

**Jessica Downham (10)**
**Ellwood Community Primary School**


## War

*What can I see? You ask.*
Bombs, planes and people trying to find
Their sons and daughters

*What can I feel? You ask.*
Achy legs and arms from dodging
Danger of gun fighting.

*What can I hear? You ask.*
Crackling fires, people screaming
And planes destroying buildings.

**Marcus Partridge (11)**
**Ellwood Community Primary School**

## Love

Love is pink like a scented rose
It sounds like my favourite record playing over and over again
Its colour is like a pink-red butterfly floating in the summer sky
It tastes like a beautiful cup of tea with a biscuit on a Friday night
It smells like a calm, scented candle
It looks like a calm river running into the ocean
It feels like a red juicy apple from the fridge
It reminds you of a sweet bird tweeting in the spring.

**Melissa Stephens (9)**
**Ellwood Community Primary School**


## War

Black bombs hit the ground then go *bang*
Bullets flying as well as shells coming out of a gun
Angry men show anger and shoot
People killing people for their lives.

**Jamie Button (10)**
**Ellwood Community Primary School**


## Anger

It sounds like a roaring monster trapped in a cave
It is purple like a witch's cloak
Fear when your mouth goes dry
It smells like a skunk in a zoo
The monster has sharp teeth and five horns
He feels like a prickly bush
It reminds me when I get angry with my sisters.

**Reece Leigh (9)**
**Ellwood Community Primary School**

## War

*What can you see?*
Innocent people dying
Bright exploding planes spinning to the ground
Bright red cartridges flying everywhere.

*What can you feel?*
Feeling lonely back at base
Very sad and painful because your friend's dying
Frightened and annoyed with yourself.

*What can you hear?*
You can hear deafening guns
Innocent people screaming
Generals shouting.

**Joshua Goldstien (10)**
Ellwood Community Primary School

## Anger

Anger is like a roaring dinosaur
It is dark red like the Devil
It tastes bitter and spicy
It looks like me fighting with my brother
It feels horrible in my heart
It reminds me of a windy storm.

**Thomas Winmill (9)**
Ellwood Community Primary School

## Water

Water smells like the horrid smell of chlorine in the pool
It sounds like pitter-patter of the rain on the window
It looks like a shiny blue wet gem glistening in the sun
It feels like a shower shooting arrows at my back
It tastes like salt and vinegar on my chips.

**Jessica Palmer (9)**
English Bicknor CE Primary School

## Water

It feels like a cold lump of snow cascading down my back
It looks like a shimmering piece of cellophane
It smells like a herbal aroma
It sounds like children playing and shouting
It tastes like Salt 'n' Shake crisps
It reminds me of waves in the bath mimicking a tsunami.

**Alice Blakemore (10)**
English Bicknor CE Primary School


## Water

It feels like icy cold shivers down my spine
It looks like shiny marbles
It smells like a fresh sunny day
It tastes like salt and vinegar crisps
It reminds me of a giant water slide.

**Charlotte Pomeroy (9)**
English Bicknor CE Primary School


## Bath Time

It looks like waves crashing in the sea
It smells like spring flowers in my garden
It sounds like pitter-patter, pitter-patter
It reminds me of a boat bobbing up and down.

**Lucy Davies (10)**
English Bicknor CE Primary School

## Waterfall

It feels like a cold blanket covering you
It sounds like a pressure washer
It looks like a stream of water pouring from a watering can
It smells like a hot steaming sauna
It tastes like condensation on a window.

**Josh Baynham (10)**
**English Bicknor CE Primary School**


## Water

It sounds like pitter-patter in a dark cave
It smells like the ocean air
It sounds like a band walking down the road
It tastes like the salt on burning chips
It reminds me of a pounding football coming towards me
It looks like smooth books in a row
It feels like the smooth metal from the cold bath
It looks like a mirror with your reflection in it
You can see bubbles from the bath tub.

**Jack Reed (10)**
**English Bicknor CE Primary School**


## Water

It looks like a clear sheet of ice
It smells like the fresh smell of a summer's day
It tastes like salt and vinegar on chips
It sounds like pitter-patter on the ground.

It reminds me of a swimming pool
It sounds like a drum beat
It feels like an ice blanket covering me.

**Guy Meredith (10)**
**English Bicknor CE Primary School**

## The Sea

What can I see?
I see calm blue water crashing along the sand
The water gleaming before my eyes
Waves pulling back from sea-battered rocks
Leaving only rings in the water behind.

What can I hear?
I hear the water crashing and splashing before the rocks
The water dripping from garbage carelessly thrown in the sea
And the whoosh of the waves flying up the shore
Leaving roaring of waves in my ears.

What can I feel?
I feel the coldness of waves when they crawl up the beach
A shiver goes up my spine
The waves wrap round my legs
Leaving the coldness with me once more.

**Becky Hone (10)**
**English Bicknor CE Primary School**


## Water

It smells like yucky water
It looks like a large, luxurious, blue blanket
It tastes like salt and vinegar crisps
It sounds like a drum in a brass band.

It smells like a really salty stew
It looks like a laminated piece of paper
It tastes like a dried piece of seaweed
It sounds like someone smashing a vase.

It smells like prawn cocktail crisps
It looks like a blue sheet like the sky
It sounds like a vacuum on the floor
It reminds me of my blue blanket across my bed.

**Matthew Jackson (10)**
**English Bicknor CE Primary School**

## Waterfall

It feels like a freezing cold ice pack
It sounds like hundreds of windows being shattered into
                                      millions of pieces
It smells like a salt cellar
It looks like broken glass exploding at the bottom of the rock face
It reminds me of thousands of marbles.

**Callum Moore (10)**
English Bicknor CE Primary School


## The Sea

It tastes like a chip with lots of salt and vinegar on top
It tastes like salt and vinegar crisps
It sounds like a twig cracking when someone's stepped on it
It sounds like the whooshing of the wind
It reminds me of the wind on top of a hill
It reminds me of a rock falling onto the floor
It looks like a huge glass mirror
It looks like a strangely shaped window
It feels like a slippery cave bottom
It feels like the wet where my shoes have been.

**Ainsley Robbins (9)**
English Bicknor CE Primary School


## Calm Sea

It tastes like salt and vinegar crisps
It sounds like washing in a machine
It feels like cold, smooth metal
It looks like a blanket of transparent glass.

**Laceyjay Wells (11)**
English Bicknor CE Primary School

## The Sea

It looks like a blue shiny sheet
It smells like damp, dark seaweed
It sounds like a squelch, squirt, swoosh and whoosh
It tastes like a bucket of salty chips
It reminds me of the shining sun
It feels like a wet worm.

**Sam Evans (10)**
English Bicknor CE Primary School


## The Seaside

It tastes like salty popcorn
It smells like chlorine in a noisy swimming pool
It looks like ripples in a swimming pool
It reminds me of the clouds on a summer day
It sounds like feet going pitter-patter
It feels like cold ice cream.

**Charlotte Butcher (8)**
English Bicknor CE Primary School


## Water

Water sounds like drip-drop, pitter-patter
And it looks like violet blue rushing down the hill
Water sounds like splish, splash, splash
And it feels slippery
Water smells like salt
And it tastes like ready salted crisps.

**Bethany Cooper (8)**
English Bicknor CE Primary School

## Water

Water looks like a thin pane of glass sparkling in the sun
It feels like a soft cuddly bed
It smells like damp seaweed
It tastes like Salt 'n' Shake crisps
It sounds like a blue tit singing.

**Harley Adams (9)**
**English Bicknor CE Primary School**


## The Sea

It tastes salty like watery vinegar on warm chips
It feels like slimy worms out of the earthy ground
I can hear the whistling of the rough wind by the wall
It sounds like glass being smashed and crashed on sharp rocks
It reminds me of jumping into a freezing cold swimming pool
It smells like fish, salty, chewy fish from the chip shop.

**Sarah Toomer (11)**
**English Bicknor CE Primary School**


## Water

It sounds like a pitter-patter on the step outside my house
It tastes like a salty pack of crisps
It looks like a laminated piece of paper
I can hear gurgling in the gutter
It feels like a cold shiver down my spine.

**Tom Barnett (10)**
**English Bicknor CE Primary School**

## The Sea

It looks like a parade of snakes dancing to the rhythm
It smells like fish
It feels like seaweed.

It tastes like salt
It reminds me of looking through the window at the sky
It sounds like someone shaking a pot with beads in.

It's fun when it's calm, but I fear it when it's mad
I love it when it's warm, but I hate it when it's cold
It brings happiness when it's happy and sadness when it's sad.

**Jeremy Hale (10)**
**English Bicknor CE Primary School**


## The Sea

It smells like sewagey, salty seaweed
It reminds me of a large, luxurious, blue blanket
It tastes like a bag of prawn cocktail crisps
It sounds like giants smashing rocks
It looks like a steaming spa.

**Amber Jenkins (10)**
**English Bicknor CE Primary School**


## Water

When it rains it sounds like someone tapping on the window
It looks like a clear, empty window
It feels like a shiver going down my spine
It reminds me of the beach.

**Jack Powell (9)**
**English Bicknor CE Primary School**

## The Sea

It sounds like trees swaying and dancing
It feels like a laminated blue sheet
It tastes like salt and vinegar crisps
It looks like a blue coat that zips.

**Catherine Larcombe (10)**
English Bicknor CE Primary School


## Sea

It sounds like a leaking pipe
It feels like a piece of silk
It looks like plain laminated paper
It tastes like fish and chips.

**Zak Williams (11)**
English Bicknor CE Primary School


## The Jaguar

The prowling jaguar, the spotty golden cat
Is hunting
In the forest, she pads stealthily, she runs, she freezes.

With beady, staring eyes near her twitching pink nose
Sensing every move of her prey
She's ready to pounce
She wriggles
Her powerful limbs show her strength
She constantly twitches and squiggles
Ready to feast on the fresh meat
Her mouth drooling at the thought
That it would be delicious.

**Ashleigh Phelps (10)**
Foxmoor CP School

## Hate Is . . .

Hate is red like a hot burning fire
Hate sounds like a bull banging inside my heart
Hate tastes like a red-hot chilli sticking to my tongue
Hate smells like grey smoke slithering up my nostrils
Hate looks like a devil slashing through my body
Hate feels like a spiky blanket wrapped right round me
Hate reminds me of a white room, empty all except for me
And all the things in this poem!

**Janneke Bax-Pratt (8)**
**Foxmoor CP School**


## Love

Love is the colour of red hearts
Love sounds like beautiful magpies up in a tree
Love tastes like sweet sugar buns
Love smells like lemon bubble bath
Love looks like a colourful rainbow
Love feels like fluffy fur from a tiger's body
Love reminds me of my little baby bunny.

**Kirsty Lawrence (9)**
**Foxmoor CP School**


## Fun Is . . .

Fun is the colour of the rainbow trying to reach the sky
Fun sounds like a laughing crowd at a fair
Fun tastes like a sherbet lemon fizzing on my tongue
Fun smells like the hot, sugary, pink, fluffy candyfloss that is
                                      waiting to be eaten
Fun looks like a playful kitten wrestling with the wool
Fun feels like soft fur rubbing on my face
Fun reminds me of happiness and laughter.

**Sophie Davis (8)**
**Foxmoor CP School**

## Life

I was born in June, the joy of my mum's life
Then she got married and became a wife
In July I had my first tooth
I got a pound under the poof.
I'm now in August, time goes so fast
Sometimes I think it will never last.
Here comes September with a smile on my face
First day of school, do up my lace
October, Hallowe'en, trick or treat to get a sweet
And now I'm at home with my brother Pete.
It's November now as fireworks go pop
Bright colours now they all stop
December passes to January as the snow is falling
Turn around Dad is calling.
February, Valentine's, giving chocolates and lockets to put pictures in
But sooner or later I'm going to put them in the bin
Now March has come, soon my life will be done
April's here with chocolate eggs
Soon I'll be hanging my washing on pegs
It's May as the swimming pool is opening
I'm now coping.

**Kiera Yam (9)**
**Foxmoor CP School**


## Love

Love is red like a flaming red heart
Love sounds like the flowers blowing in the wind
Love tastes like a red cherry growing from a tree
Love smells like a romantic meal on a plate
Love looks like a hill with chocolate on
Love feels like the smoothness of a red rose
Love reminds me of a beautiful tropical island.

**Regan Garraway (8)**
**Foxmoor CP School**

## The Iguana

The camouflaged iguana,
In the leafy undergrowth
Is lost
In the rainforest, he walks, he pounds, he stomps.

With sharp spikes coming up from his tail to his back
Sticking into animals flesh, to protect himself from his prey
He wanders round the undergrowth
Catching small beasts with his long tongue.

He can't hunt any prey!
He wanders all around but still can't find his prey.
He lies starving where the sun doesn't beam with its sunlight
He cannot walk any longer, dying of hunger
He waits, he waits, he waits.

**Kacey Garraway (10)**
**Foxmoor CP School**


## Fun Is . . .

Fun is a rainbow reaching the flaming hot sun
Fun sounds like laughter here and happiness there
Fun, it tastes like sweet, strong chocolate flying in the air
Fun smells like a steaming hot pudding waiting to be eaten
Fun looks like people playing all day long
Fun feels like bubbles floating in my tummy
Fun reminds me of a circus.

**Samantha Haughton (8)**
**Foxmoor CP School**

## Deforestation Of The Pygmy Owl

The pygmy owl, the devastated bird
Is flying for the first time
He's in the air, he lowers, he lowers again.

His claws grip something, horrible thoughts that it's another animal
Waiting to eat him
He opens his eyes slowly
Blinking once or twice to make sure the tree isn't an illusion
He realises he's made it to another tree
But when he flies back, waiting for his family to congratulate him
He reveals a piece of the rainforest missing, including his home
Sadly he finds a dozen birds
Lying dead on the forest floor
*Oh,* he thinks, *is this my family?*

The pygmy owl
A sad and homeless bird
Is crying for the first time.
He coughs, he splutters, he weeps.
Who has done this?
Why did they do it?

**Charlotte Cowley (9)**
**Foxmoor CP School**


## Respect

R espect all living things around us
E scape rudeness and naughtiness
S hare feelings and friends
P lease don't hurt people's feelings
E ject all alcohol and drugs
C onnect goodness to everyone
T reat people how you would like to be treated.

**Molly Bale (10)**
**Foxmoor CP School**

## Hunger

Hunger is blank like a big piece of paper
Hunger sounds like your tummy rumbling in the middle of the night
Hunger tastes like an empty bowl waiting to be filled
Hunger smells like rotten fish
Hunger's a bad dream that haunts me.

**Alys Chitty (9)**
**Foxmoor CP School**


## I Wonder Why . . .

I wonder why the grass is green
I wonder why my clothes are clean
I wonder why cars are fast
I wonder why I'm always last
I wonder why cats are soft
I wonder why we have a loft

I wonder why we take photos
I wonder why we have a nose
I wonder why we wear shoes
I wonder why police need clues
I wonder why we have names
I wonder why we like games

I wonder why we need air
I wonder why we always care
I wonder why we watch telly
I wonder why we eat jelly
I wonder why I was born
I wonder why we play on the lawn

I wonder why we have soft pets
I wonder why my gramp's dog's Bets
I wonder why we toast bread
I wonder why my ball's red
I wonder why my room's a mess
Oh, well, I'll just never guess!

**Ellena Brown (9)**
**Foxmoor CP School**

## Silence Is . . .

Silence is the colour of white clouds waiting to land
Silence is a sound like an empty room waiting for sound
Silence is a taste like a pancake with no sugar
Silence is a smell like a plain crisp with no salt at all
Silence looks like an empty playground waiting for children to come
Silence feels like a cold breeze blowing against your body
Silence reminds me of my house when no one's home.
*Empty!*

**Jordan Grant (8)**
Foxmoor CP School

## What Has Happened To Lulu?

Has she got kidnapped, Mother?
Has she run away?
Has someone taken her, Mother?
Will I see Loo again?

Who was it that came last night?
Was it to do with her?
Was it really a dream last night?
Please tell me Mother, I miss her Mum I do!

**Charis Wyatt (9)**
Foxmoor CP School

## A Toothbrush Dreams

A toothbrush dreams of singing,
Of opening up the bristly ends
And singing like a pop star at the top of the charts
it dreams of being popular in an opera in New York
Singing with Fifty Cent
It dreams of a voice that would be dreamed by other people
It wishes it could wear Elvis' suit with a rocking Afro
Unfortunately it's not even got a voice!

**Jefferson Thomas (10)**
Foxmoor CP School

## Love

Love is a red heart beating in the sky
Love sounds like two dicky birds making music on the wall
Love tastes like a chocolate pudding kiss
Love smells like sweet flowers in the sunshine
Love looks like wind dancing in the air
Love reminds me of my family.

**Aiesha Williams (8)**
**Foxmoor CP School**


## Sadness

Sadness is light blue like tears from your eyes
Sadness sounds like a crying orphan wishing for her family
Sadness tastes like a blank cup cake so horrible and boring
Sadness smells like a red rose with no scent
Sadness feels like a tree with no leaves
Sadness looks like a lonely oak tree
Sadness reminds me of an orphan.

**Zoe Smith (8)**
**Foxmoor CP School**


## My Anaconda

He slithers
He smells
He goes to Mum and tells

He's smart
He's a good piece of art
He's like a fast little dart

He's hairy
He's lairy
He's really very scary.

**Sam Coates (9)**
**Foxmoor CP School**

## Fun Is . . .

Fun is a strong, metallic blue shining on the horizon
Fun is the sound of laughter ringing in my ears
Fun is the taste of a lollipop swirling with different colours
Fun is the smell of a bunch of roses blooming from the ground
Fun looks like children running everywhere
Fun feels like a soft sponge caressing your gentle skin
Fun reminds me of playing in the sun
. . . And fun is exactly like . . . *me!*

**Lianne Burnell (8)**
**Foxmoor CP School**


## Snakes

The slithering, slimy snake
Its colour reflects in the sun like a rainbow
They're big noises like a bang from a gun
They're axes chopping down homes
They have massive cages for animals to take for money
They are greedy for animals to make things for money
*Bang, bang, bang,* the snake is dead,
There soon will be nothing left at all.

**Danielle Berry (9)**
**Foxmoor CP School**


## Anger

Anger is the colour of red burning wildly
Anger sounds like a huge troll roaring madly
Anger tasted like a hot chilli burning on my tongue
Anger smells like burning rock shooting out of a volcano
Anger looks like a red tree growing in my eyes
Anger feels like a red bull banging in my head wanting to get out
Anger reminds me of an angry monster smashing walls.

**Adam Gloyne (8)**
**Foxmoor CP School**

## My Life

You were born in June with the sun at your side
Already your mouth was learning to glide.

You thought about the doll's house with the little wooden door,
Your heart full of joy and already your love starting to soar.

And when August came, you were shouting out in vain
For a brother or sister to play with in the rain.

You went to school in September, times happened good and bad,
The bullies you tried not to remember, but in the end you were glad.

The time came when you left, everyone started to moan and groan,
You packed your stuff and left with a gruff.

December came and the snow fell down,
You went to the circus and saw a clown.

Snow fell on the floor, a man came knocking on the door.
January with the year so white, as the paper you're writing on at
                                                  the dead of night.

**Rowan Duval-Fryer (9)**
**Foxmoor CP School**


## Help!

R is for the raindrops dripping from the trees
A is for the ants crawling in the leaves
I is for the iguana who's changing colour against the bark
N is for the nocturnal creatures waking up when it's dark
F is for the forest floor covered in leaves, plants and creepy-crawlies
O is for the orang-utan swinging high between the tops of trees
R is for the murky rivers which flow through the forests to the sea
E is for all the endangered species that may soon no longer be
S is for all the snakes lying in wait for their prey
T is for the number of trees that are being destroyed every day
S is for *save our rainforest!*
   *Don't cut down all the trees please!*

**Victoria Cullen (9)**
**Foxmoor CP School**

## People

Where are the people?
Where did they go?
Are they up in Heaven
Or under the ground?
They've disappeared in the mist
And never returned
What has happened to them Mother?
What has happened to the people?
Have they gone on their holiday or to the beach?
Did they leave their dogs behind or give them a treat?
Mother, now you've disappeared, you never know
I or you might be next!

**Alice Samways (10)**
**Foxmoor CP School**

## Help, Let Me Go

I was lying, lying on the fresh grass
Looking around for help
That's all I needed
But I can't, too helpless to yelp
I tried, tried to get up
To run out of this trap
Lost, lost forever
They had the map
Crying, crying with fear
They had caught me
I knew I was lost now
Shivering, I'm in need of warm tea
My heart was pumping, pumping faster
My mind went coldly blank
My head was dizzy
Though my body lay there, I was free.

**Rachael Boddington (10)**
**Hopelands School**

## The Sound Collector
*(Based on 'The Sound Collector' by Roger McGough)*

The milkman came this morning
Dressed all in black and white,
Scooped all the sounds into a bottle
And took them to the greatest height.

The pouring of the milk
The clatter of the spoons,
The sawing of the bread
The wind wrapping round the moon.

The purring of the kitten
The hissing of the gas,
The whistling of the kettle
The smashing of the glass.

The rustling of the paper
When the pages turn,
The noise of the smoke alarm
When the toast began to burn.

The milkman came this morning
He didn't leave his name,
Left us only in silence
Life will never be the same.

**Emily Walker-Smith (11)**
Hopelands School

## I Am

I am a dove full of peace
I am a cheeky monkey swinging in trees
I am a yo-yo bouncing and laughing
I am a bright yellow sun full of light
I am a ripe banana ready to burst out
I am a tidal wave big and strong
I am a sticky doughnut you will find the best bit inside.

**Lydia Gray (10)**
Hopelands School

## Me And My Piano

Oh to play on the piano again,
The notes I love to hear.
The keys shine like moonbeams sparkling so clear.
All I ask is a small room to play and practise in
With a soft cushion on a wooden stool
To keep my books within.

Oh to play on the piano again,
Watching my fingers dancing
Moving over the keys until they sing, so enchanting.
The low notes sound like the beat of a drum
The high notes make me want to hum
*Rum ti tum ti tum ti tum.*

Oh to play on the piano again,
The tune that plays and sways
With the music I play with ease.
My piano is all that matters to me
And I'd love one of my own
I'd play in schools, I'd play at shows,
But it's best when I'm all alone!

**Emily Ham (8)**
**Hopelands School**

## The Dog

A friendly companion is the dog
It sometimes wallows in the bog.

It jumps up at its lead
To show you that it wants to be freed.

Its eyes light up like a Christmas tree
It jumps up then you very kindly agree.

Suddenly it meets another dog
It runs around and leaps over a log.

But when it's had quite enough
It goes away in a stroppy huff.

**Alice Lord (8)**
**Hopelands School**

## My Gelert

O' Gelert! My Gelert!
You murdered my baby prince,
How could you? I loved you, well maybe just a tince,
You wicked dog! You evil dog!
I'll get you back on this,
The sword drove through Gelert's throat,
For a cry! A yelp! a heartbreak note,
O' but horror! Horror! Horror!
A trickle, sleek and red,
For on the floor my Gelert lies,
Murdered, bitter and dead.

O' Gelert! My Gelert!
You faithful, gentle hound,
Forgive me, you're gone,
For the dreadful thing I've done,
I thank you dearly, for saving my baby prince,
The wolf, you killed him,
He's vanished and very dim,
But O horror! Horror! Horror!
O' draining blots on your head,
For on the floor my Gelert lies,
Murdered, bitter and dead.

**Alice Barber (9)**
**Hopelands School**


## Waraphobia

I am scared of World War III
Like a surfboard is scared of drowning
Like snow is petrified of melting
Like a teddy is terror-stricken of no love
Like a clock is anxious to stop ticking
Like a memory is shocked at forgetting
I am scared of World War III.

**Grace Barber (10)**
**Hopelands School**

## Her Senses

She opened her eyes and saw nothing
Except the bombed buildings
Except the black sky
Except dead bodies

She heard nothing
Except the shooting of the guns
Except the howling of the wounded
Except the crying of the children

She felt nothing
Except the emptiness which lay at the pit of her stomach
Except the tears falling down her cheeks
Except the thumping in her head

She thought of nothing
Except the bitterness that filled her that day
Except the way her parents died
Except, except *everything*.

**Siobhan Bradburn (10)**
**Hopelands School**


## O' Teacher! My Teacher

O' teacher! My teacher, with long golden hair
Give me my pencil, I promise I will share!
I will do all my homework in ten minutes flat
I will let you relax and even train your cat!

O' teacher! My teacher, all the work is done
I can even say sometimes my homework can be fun!
My work on the Egyptians hangs proudly on the wall
I sit and do my French words and do not mind at all!

O' teacher! My teacher, the long day is done
Now give me my pencil and I'll run, run, run!

**Alice Bloomer (8)**
**Hopelands School**

## Me

I am a huge T-rex, teeth bared,
I am an Egyptian text book, overflowing with knowledge,
I am the colour red, bristling with anger,
I am a bookworm, head buried,
I am a fiery elephant, tusks ripping, feeling flat,
I am a ford gobbler, devouring all,
I am a volcano, ready to erupt.

**Tom O'Dell (11)**
**Hopelands School**


## My Bunny Honey

I once had a bunny,
Her name was Honey.
She was a rabbit,
With a very bad habit.
She was no ordinary pet,
She was always at the vet.
She liked to have fights,
With pairs of my mum's tights.
She'd get all tangled,
As in the tights she dangled.
It would take hours for her to chew,
All of the tights through.
She knew it was a mistake,
When she had tummy ache.
She'd often spend the night,
At the vet's because of tights.
Alas, my bunny Honey,
When she was eleven,
She went to bunny Heaven.

**Emily Hepworth (9)**
**Kempsford CE Primary School**

## Stars

On dark, clear nights,
I look out of my bedroom window
And I can see hundreds of stars,
Bright stars, light stars, twinkling back at me,
Shooting stars and sparkling stars
And I can see the moon too,
Shaped like an enormous banana,
Floating in the sky.

**Alex Britt (7)**
**Kempsford CE Primary School**


## My Family

My auntie Bacterial, anti-bacterial
Was made from chemicals and special material.
She won't eat pie, she won't eat toast,
She won't even eat Sunday roast.

My uncle Soap, uncle Soap,
Went to the zoo to wash the antelope.
Some say he's crazy, others say he's keen,
But most of all he's blooming clean.

My tidy mum, Mum tidy,
Went to the tidy club on Friday.
She'll tidy anything in sight,
That's when I got home, it gave me a fright.

My dusty dad, dusty dad,
Throws his dust around so he's bad.
Some say he's dusty, others say he should live in a bin,
But most of all they say his son takes after him.

My dirty brother, brother dirty,
Always has a mucky shirty.
For he spreads his mud in a trail,
When it comes to mud he will never fail!

**Giselle Failes (11)**
**Kingswood Primary School**

## Spy (Disguised)

It may not be particularly wise
But it's a thrill to be disguised
Hiding in, hiding out,
Looking to see if there's a criminal about
Looking left, looking right,
Looking around day and night.
Hearing screams of stolen lace
I say don't worry I'm on the case.
I look with my glasses, I look with my eyes,
I cover my body in an amazing disguise.
I write in my notebook, I take a close look
I walk around and discover what he took
Sometimes I tell a humongous lie
But overall it's really great fun to be a spy
It may not be particularly wise,
But it's a thrill to be disguised!

**Olivia Harper (10)**
**Kingswood Primary School**


## The Earth's Diamond

Orange like the sun
Blue as the skies
The cavities, the springs
Growing even hotter
The pathways of man
Winding with nature
Colours, textures ever brighter
Nature's working its charm on you
Green, yellow, orange and blue
The rainbow's fallen down to Earth
Lava escaping from its enemies
The Earth's diamond set in the rock
Slowly dissolving, destroyed by man.

**Polly Clare-Hudson (9)**
**Kingswood Primary School**

## Dragon's Life

Its scaly wings beating loud,
High and mighty, very proud.
Burning anything in its path,
Scorching people who dare laugh.
Stealing sheep from innocent farms,
Wrenching off the roofs of barns.
Yet this seems not to satisfy,
As it looks through its diamond eye.
Sees nothing but what it has done,
Yet only wanting to love someone
So do you think this beast is bad?

**Michael Rowe (10)**
**Kingswood Primary School**


## Special Spring - Haiku

Bright patterned flowers
Artists scattered paint palette
Grand, green, growing grass.

**Katie Smith (10)**
**Kingswood Primary School**


## The Hunt

What did I do to deserve this?
I wasn't the one who stole the chick
And now you're tearing me bit by bit.

Why do you hunt me day by day?
I try to escape and run away
My cubs are calling me under the tree
But now the angel of death has taken me.

**Lottie Aldridge (9)**
**Kingswood Primary School**

# The Wonders Of Winter

My wonders are the wonders of winter,
November,
the fireworks are my wonders,
they spring up like sprouting spring snowdrops,
mauve, cream, blue, green and dramatic red,
then roasted chestnuts, hot and roasted,
cosy inside the barn,
December,
one of my favourite months,
it's Christmas,
lots of pressies wrapped up
in shiny red and green wrapping paper,
I rip one open,
my favourite thing,
Christmas lunch,
the best Christmas pud,
on Boxing Day the hunt we watch
gallop through the fields frosty,
January,
beautiful snowdrops,
daffodil bulbs, buds and aconites,
sprouting, looking up at the bright sun,
and lastly my favourite,
February, my birthday month,
I can't wait, lots of presents,
wrapped up in rough brown paper,
my winter, a beautiful wonder!

**Lucy Dowling (10)**
**Kitebrook House School**

## Voyage Of The Planets

The sun's luminous glare suffuses the dim atmosphere
Mercury, scorching with violent heat.
Venus, exhaling her toxic gas and entrancing any object with
                                                               her beauty.
Earth, sharing secrets with life
Mars, crimson with boldness flashes his might.
Jupiter with his regal power reigns over his planetary subjects.
Saturn, ambushed by moons.
Uranus, down with depression of drought.
Neptune, bathed in cerulean blue, entertains the solar system.
Pluto, his gloomy entity skulks over the universe.

**Antonia Dalivalle (10)**
**Kitebrook House School**

## Horses For Courses

Stamping and snorting and ready to race
They all set off and the fillies set the pace.
They chase to the first and all pile over
Some of them fall, others throw their jockeys over.
They run to the next with their jockeys pressing ahead
Some refuse to jump, but most carry on instead.
Their colours are bright
In the spring sunlight
As they race each other for the first place home.

Galloping horses and gripping jockeys race
Trying to win the very first place.
They race every week in the racing season
The jockeys choose who to ride with one good reason
To win the title of the leading man
Several try, but only one can.
Horses for courses, if that's the case
Why do they win in a different place?

**Pandora Fowles (10)**
**Kitebrook House School**

# Horses

Horses gallop through the countryside,
Horses have their ears pricked,
Tails high,
Heads high,
Twinkle in their eyes.
Their mane and tail is flowing,
They love the breezy air,
The leader of the herd is a bay thoroughbred,
Who is very fair,
He leads them through Wales, Gloucestershire and York.

At night he stands guard,
Tail high,
Head high,
Twinkle in his eye.
Sometimes they watch the morning hunt,
They sometimes even follow.

Most of the mares have foals,
Palominos and Welsh mountains.
When it is snowing,
There are icicles on the trees
The sun shines in them,
Like a chandelier.
In stormy weather,
The bay thoroughbred rounds up the herd,
They all gallop home to safety.

**Henrietta Trevelyan (10)**
**Kitebrook House School**

## Teacher's Pet

My teacher has lots of pets
And I'm not one of them.
Sophie, Miranda and Lucy
You have no idea
What's the mayhem!

Sophie is a snake
Miranda is a duck,
Lucy is a koala bear
Snooty and stuck up.

Sophie tried to strangle me
When I got full marks
Lucy is very silly
Once she tried to bark!

Miranda sits on my desk
So I cannot work
Sophie is quite lazy
Rolling herself round Lucy's perch.

My teacher has lots more pets
I daren't say it
Our classroom is such a mess
Because it is a spider's nest!

**Isobel Styler (9)**
**Kitebrook House School**

## The Snow Pony

The pony was a dapple grey
On the mountain ledge.

Its grey mane blowing in the foggy mist
It was standing in the snow
Its fetlocks fluffy and very thin.

Dapple-grey pony
On the mountain ledge.

Gallops down towards me
As if to say, 'I'm hungry.
Please give me something to eat.'

Dapple-grey pony
On the mountain ledge.

Its eyes were wide
Its nostrils were flared.

Dapple-grey pony on the mountain ledge.

**Chloe O'Kane (9)**
**Kitebrook House School**


## The Pony In The Snow

It was then when I saw him
A snow-white horse
Galloping in and out
Of his herd of snow-white horses
And ponies on the sand,
The sand, sand was flying in the air
It looked as if they were taking off
Into the midnight air
And then they vanished.

**Imogen Gloag (9)**
**Kitebrook House School**

# Winter

Frost is the king of winter.
His face is as white as an Arctic fox dressed in a silver cloak
His long white hair streams behind him.
As his billowing cloak touches the ground
The grass suddenly turns to ice.
He raises his hands to turn all the raindrops to icicles
Winter moans as he hardens the ground
He scatters diamonds as he goes.
Winter paints a beautiful picture of the distant hills and the fog
He sprinkles the frost on gate posts and fences.
Winter undresses all the trees as he savagely winds in and out
And as he goes he spreads a snowy carpet over the grass.

**Matilda Jacobs (8)**
**Kitebrook House School**


# Cold

Winter is cold
My breath freezes
My fingers are frozen numb.

When I breathe
I look like a dragon
Catching snowflakes on my tongue.

The road is as slippery as can be
Field like a blanket of snow
The wind is a roaring lion.

The robin puffs up for warmth
Ducks look like they are skating on ice.

Snow crunches under my feet
People in the streets have chattering teeth
Even the snowman shivers.

**Francesca White (9)**
**Kitebrook House School**

## Hallowe'en

'Trick or treat?' comes the chorus,
Chocolate falls into their bags,
And the cackling 'witches' run away.

Midnight strikes - the witching hour,
The babble of voices dies down
All is quiet.

The door creaks and my spine prickles
The stench of rotting flesh fills the room
The light from the pumpkin flickers and dies
A ghastly presence, blacker than black,
Has suddenly entered the room.

This awful being will not rest
Until its ghostly thirst is quenched
Silence echoes round the room.

The darkness fades and melts away
The lights come on
Where is the host of the party?
The mystery's yet to be solved
But stay in bed on Hallowe'en
Or you'll meet with horrors untold.

**Polly Hughes (10)**
**Kitebrook House School**

## A Roar As An Echo

Deep in the jungle lies the lion's cave
Which all animals dread
If they go in they'll soon be dead
Fearful of the lion's roar as an echo . . . echo . . . echo.

The lion's roar makes the walls shiver
The mice flee their homes
All to be seen in the jungle is new and old bones
As all the animals are high in trees, camouflaged or down in holes
Terrified of the lion's roar as an echo . . . echo . . . echo.

The animals so scared want to rid the jungle of the lion
So they take revenge by a plan
And went to find the great god Pan
So they could be free from the lion's roar as an echo . . . echo
. . . echo.

The great god Pan's plan worked
The lion was tricked to fall into his own den
By the reflection of a hen.

So the animals are now happy in the wood
They are freed from what felt like a long winter to hibernate
Now there is no lion to make the roar as an echo . . . echo . . . echo.

**Charlotte Mills (10)**
**Kitebrook House School**

# Through The Eyes Of A Blind Child

My touch is precious,
It feels for me,
The warmth of a hand,
The cold of a fridge,
But still, I see nothing.

I hear the birds,
Sing their sweet song,
The soft breeze rushes
Against my face,
But still, I see nothing.

I smell the scent,
Of flowers which grow,
The smell of dewed grass,
Like diamonds beneath the sea,
But still, I see nothing.

I taste the tang of fresh fruit,
The juice full of taste and sweetness,
But still, I see nothing.

Suddenly, there is a bright light,
The touch of love,
From the fingers of a mother
Then I see something.

**Piera Van de Wiel (10)**
**Kitebrook House School**

## The Tsunami

The tsunami appeal,
Was a great, great deal,
The tide went high,
But then went low,
To and fro
Again and again.

I saw it all happen
People swept out to sea
Most of whom lost their homes
Children have lost their parents
They have tears
Running down their faces.

People in devastation
Knowing they are gone
Gone forever and ever
Innocent lives ruined
People never to be seen again.

Boxing Day the very day
The devastation happened
Cars swept out
People on the beach couldn't run
It happened so quickly,
Lives, families
Swept away and away
Never seen since.

**Lara Fenton (10)**
**Kitebrook House School**

# The Netball Match

It's Friday night,
I've had my dream,
I'm on the list!
I've made the team!

I'm goal attack
My favourite place
I mustn't slack,
I must shoot straight.

We're on the coach,
We're ready to go,
We're all very keen
But nervous of the foe!

The coach arrives,
The team is there,
They're all very big,
That isn't fair!

The whistle goes,
We've got the ball,
It's passed to me,
I score a goal!

It's close to finishing,
We don't want a draw,
One more goal
And we could win!

One minute to go,
A penalty throw,
I've got the ball,
It's in the net!

**India Case (10)**
**Kitebrook House School**

## My Life Has No Excitement

My life has no excitement
I go to school each day
I work at my desk
And try my best
But things never go my way.

Things that would excite me
Double art each day
Getting the part I want in the play;
I wish things went my way.

I'd love to have my dog back
But Mum sent him away
She said he was a pain in the butt
I wish things went my way.

I wish it would just snow non-stop
So I could go and play
Build a snowman as big as me
I wish things went my way.

I wish I had a mansion
With no big bills to pay
A hundred acres to keep my horses
I wish things went my way.

If things went my way all the time
I'd be a spoilt brat
So perhaps things should just stay as they are
So I should wish for something simpler than that.

**Emily Liggins (10)**
**Kitebrook House School**

## The Mare And The Foal

The mare has had a foal
The foal is opening its eyes to a whole new world
It is unsteady, but soon balances.

Its mother soon shows it where to go
After a while it can walk and then trot and then canter.

**Courtney Ferguson (9)**
**Kitebrook House School**


## Snow

Snow is so magical to me
As everything is so different
All around is white
With no single footstep in sight.

When snow falls
It looks like cotton wool
But it feels so wet and cold
That I know to wrap up warm.

Snow on trees looks like fairy land
So I pretend that is where I am
I tiptoe across the white carpet
Thinking of another magic land.

Then suddenly the sun comes out
And everything begins to melt
My dreams are all ruined
As the snow begins to go.

**Isobel Kenny-Herbert (10)**
**Kitebrook House School**

## Winter

Winter rolled over the misty moorland
He called the stream to a halt
Carefully he picked each leaf and drove it to the ground
Leaving skull-like figures towering in the darkness
Each blade of grass froze as winter passed the garden boundary
And his breath howled over the icy fields.

**Bunny Cockerton-Airy (8)**
**Kitebrook House School**


## Mum Said No!

It was snowing today
I said to my family hip, hip, hooray
I rushed outside to play in the snow
And then Mum said, 'No!'

I went to the fair tonight
The candyfloss was a tempting sight
I headed to buy some I wasn't slow
But Mum said, 'No!'

I wanted to build a house in the trees
I thought I could climb with incredible ease
But when I was high she panicked below
And Mum said, 'No!'

I decided to tidy my room today
I didn't go out and I didn't play
So clean and so tidy it did gleam and glow
Then Mum said, 'Oh!'

**Lottie Carron (10)**
**Kitebrook House School**

## The Tsunami

It came and it went, but when it went,
It took more than a million people
It took lives, it took souls and people's houses
But it went too fast and it went with people.

No one knew it was going to happen,
No one knew the pain it would cause,
But out there right now
People are living and people are dying.

It wrecked houses, it killed families,
It murdered countries, we have lost so many people
So please give money to help them live again
They deserve a life again, they deserve a home again.

The wave came, the wave went,
Taking with it English people, foreign people
All sorts of people, each a glimpse and gone forever.

**Lucy Sloane (10)**
**Kitebrook House School**


## Alone

I'm all alone in the world
All alone I say
My mum and dad are gone
It must be my turn next
The tractor's coming nearer
Petrol fills my lungs
I'm the only tree for miles
So many animals gone
Axes raised
It's over, over I say
I'm lying in a forest
A pile of rotting wood
It's the end, the end I say.

**Madeleine Allardice (10)**
**Kitebrook House School**

## Wind When I Am In Bed

When my window is wide open at night
I slide under the cover to hide from the fright
For the night winds howl like a sky ghost's cry.

I cuddle up close to my teddy's paw
To hope for the spring breeze to come through my door
Shadows creep up from the light in the hall.

A cold gale blows off my cover with ease
And leaves me naked in the pitch-black room to tease
All my toys turn into monsters and roar.

The night is ended and all is peaceful
The sun has woken and shines its light on the hill
It has invited the bird to be heard.

At last I can feel my spring breeze feeling
Up in the clear blue sky of the early morning
But oh what horrors will I face the next night?

**Ingrid Straume-Brown (11)**
**Kitebrook House School**


## The Night Stallion

Flames are leaping and night is creeping
Still we fly on
For my steed and I will never cling
The speed of the dark night winds
We will be blown by the breeze
And the wind in the trees
We will canter in the skies
Then dawn has come
Day has begun
A stable of pearly-white cloud
For I am the night wind
I am the night rain
I am the night itself.

**Helen Stewart (9)**
**Kitebrook House School**

# Sea Ghosts

A creak, a slam, a swish of a coat
Is all I heard in the dark, big boat
The deep sea rippling all around
When storms brew up there is no sound
Until one night I heard a drone
A whisper nearby and soft footsteps
A scared scream from a sad, lost sailor
Somewhere in the cream coloured mist
And then the ship started to turn
Softly then roughly
Quietly then loudly
I went up on deck
To see a crew of 40 ghosts
Sailing the sea,
The sea,
The sea,
Sailing the sea
The ghosts were sailing the sea.

**Lucy Colquhoun (11)**
**Kitebrook House School**

## Three Wild Stallions

The stallions arrived here six years ago
One was black, one was bay and the other no one knows
The black one was evil
The bay one was bold
And the other one we found out was piebald
The other day one of them broke the fence
The black one even jumped the hedge
The stallions became worse and worse
No one could calm them down
Every horse bucks and every horse rears
But these ones were above my ears
The stallions would bolt and career around
No mole hill mounds would be left
But six years later a horse box arrived
And took the stallions away
I was quite upset (and nobody knows)
But I haven't seen them since
Phew!

**Georgia Wood (9)**
**Kitebrook House School**

## Winter

In winter
The wind sweeps
The crackling leaves off
The frozen floor.

In winter
The rain glides delicately
Down a misty windowpane.

In winter
The frost paints a freezing
Picture of moonlight
Which glistens like stars above.

In winter
The cold runs into the air
Like a river
And dances as it flies.

In winter
The icy-cold breath of a fox
Dissolves in the air
Like the snow in water.

In winter
Snowflakes glint as they fall
On the ground
Forming a crystal carpet.

In winter
The mysterious fog
Covers the surroundings
As the star-shaped snowflakes fall.

**Isabella Grive (8)**
**Kitebrook House School**

## Smuggler Toby

I can hear the rushing waves
Clashing against my boat
Like a horse's metal hooves
I can hear in the inn people's clashing cups
The rowing of drunken sailors
I can taste the salty sand flying in my mouth.

I can smell the salty sea
I can smell the smoke of cigarettes
I can smell the salty sand
I can feel the howling wind rushing against my skin.

I can feel myself sweating
I can see the people rowing
And some others bowing
I can see the rocking boats
And some that just float
I am funny but sly
And I love my pie
With a glint in my eye.

**Martha Hicks (10)**
**Nailsworth CE Primary School**


## Smuggler's Song

One gloomy night in the pitch-black street
Who knows what you might meet.

If you hear a trot, do not look out the window
Because they might come and smuggle you
I'd rather stay in that bed if I were you.

**Liam Close (10)**
**Nailsworth CE Primary School**

## Warning

When I am an woman
I shall wear purple pyjamas in every shop
And sing noisy songs on the bus
And sit in the middle of the road
And cause road accidents.

I shall spend my pension on sweets
And fill boots with custard
And fill balloons with cream and pop them over
Babies and make them cry.
I shall eat chips and kick people in the shins
And never say I'm sorry.
And set off fire alarms and zoom down the street
On my granny mobile.
I shall write graffiti on my neighbour's walls.
And on Hallowe'en I shall trick or treat
And when I get my sweets or money
I will throw plums at everyone.

But maybe I ought to practise a little now?
So people who know me are not too shocked and surprised
When suddenly I am old and start to wear purple pyjamas in
every shop.

**Pippa Welch (10)**
**Northleach CE Primary School**


## Where I Lie

I lie here beneath Flanders fields.
Above me, scattered poppies are swaying elegantly,
Where once there were bodies scattered carelessly.
The poppies peer over the dead bodies,
Giving hope to our families.

I lie here beneath Flanders fields.

**Emily Creed (10)**
**Northleach CE Primary School**

## So I Am Still Lying Here

So I am still lying here after all this time
Each year the poppies come back
Back like blood
Blood of the soldiers.

So I am still lying here after all this time
Each year the poppies come back
I did not want to go to war
My family and friends were scared.

So I am still lying here after all this time
Each year the poppies come back
And now I am scared
What will happen to my family?

So we are still here after all this time
Each year the poppies come back
So wear them with pride.

**Stephanie Powell (11)**
**Northleach CE Primary School**


## Poppy Love

Let us be in peace, not war.
Non-stop every day.
Remember those who went to war and died for us
All the time, day after day, men died for our country.
Let us be friends, not enemies.
For poppies are the only standing flower in Flanders field.
Let us live our lives, not die because of the war.
Let's live our lives in peace not at war
Remember peace, not war.

**Nicholas Basson (11)**
**Northleach CE Primary School**

# Warning!

When I am an old woman I will become a Goth
And hang garlic from my ceiling in my bedroom
And I shall wink at younger men with a devilish smile
And wear my curlers to Tesco's for a laugh.
I shall pretend I am a rally driver in my scooter
And pinch lollies from toddlers and children
And become a model wearing only stilettos
And occasionally underwear.
I shall breathe on people when I've got a cold
And give slobbery kisses
And learn to skateboard.

But maybe I ought to practise a little now?
So people who know me aren't too shocked and surprised
When suddenly I am old and start to wear black.

**Cait Bleakley (10)**
**Northleach CE Primary School**


# We Will Never Forget

I remember the day
The day that no one forgets,
That day that changed our lives
And that none of us will regret.
The time they risked their lives for us
For our safety and peace,
The horror, the fury and violence
That led to this day.
The blood-red poppy of hope
That lived through those years of fear
And now the flag flies high with pride
For the people we will never forget.

**Imogen Deacon (11)**
**Northleach CE Primary School**

## We Remember The Soldiers

We remember the soldiers who fought in Flanders fields,
We retain the feelings of soldiers,
Who lost their friends,
Who survived,
Who died.

We commemorate the people who were risked to save us,
Who fell on the poppies
Which grew through the fighting,
On Flanders fields,
Where bodies grew like poppies.

The poppies showed hope,
The poppies showed happiness,
The poppies showed life,
The poppies showed love.

**Paige Yates (11)**
**Northleach CE Primary School**


## A Poppy For Life

Remember the time the soldiers fought for us,
The time they died for us to give us freedom.
Everywhere in Flanders fields are scattered poppies
Where the brave men once lay.

Thanks to them we live the life that we live today
Not praying for a better life in the hope for another chance.

We should thank them for what they did
As friends they fought their foe
And every year the spirits on the 11th hour of the 11th day
Of the 11th month
Come out to battle again.

**Rosemary Webb (11)**
**Northleach CE Primary School**

# Warning

When I'm an old man I will wear fish on my head
And I will sit on other people's motorbikes
And take forever crossing the road and stop in the middle
And I shall trip up little kids and make them cry.
I shall test out new ringtones in the cinema
And break into TV stations and pull funny faces!
And buy all my shopping in pennies
And go to the shops just in my pants.
I shall lie on the road and put ketchup on my head
And pinch other people's shopping.
I might start now so people aren't so shocked
When suddenly I'm old and start to wear fish on my head.

**Jamie Fisher (11)**
**Northleach CE Primary School**


# That Tragic Day

We remember a day
    That day was tragic.
It changed our lives forever
    Soldiers were carried out to war.
To fight for our country
    We remember the gunfire.
That killed the soldiers
    In Flanders fields.
Blood was spilt
    Telegrams were sent.
To families hoping they would come back
    After the war.
Poppies covered the field
    As red as blood.
We wear poppies
    To remember.
Those who fought
    We remember a day
That was tragic.

**Ashley Nash (11)**
**Northleach CE Primary School**

## Warning!

When I am an old woman I shall
Be sick on people and run away
And I shall go to an art gallery
And break a vase.
I shall wear pink shoes with
Green trousers in Tesco's
And scream in people's ears
And I shall play the clarinet at
2 o'clock in the morning.
I shall spend my pension on
Knickers that aren't my size.

I shall grow hair
Under my armpits
And wear loads of earrings
And I will go into hospital and
Fake being ill.
I shall go on a live show and
Pull faces in front of the
Camera.

But maybe I ought to practice a
Little now?
So people who know me are not too
Shocked and surprised
When suddenly I am old and I'm
Sick on people and run away.

**Shelley Larner (10)**
**Northleach CE Primary School**

## When We Fought Amongst The Poppies

When we fought amongst the poppies
We thought, *let's give them a future.*
They will fill their hearts with the love
And hope the poppies bring them.

Poppies mean the colour of red,
The colour of blood and the life
We carelessly left behind us.
They will live their lives to the full.

We won and survived for the country,
In battlefields we showed no fear
To them who kept no peace,
We taught them to keep the peace.

We have learned to keep the peace
We did not want to go to battle
Let's make friends and keep the peace
We killed if you threatened us.

We now lay there amongst the poppies,
Thinking out our past and present.
We think about our children's future
And hope their hearts will be full of love.

**Jennifer Powell (11)**
**Northleach CE Primary School**


## Going To School

I see my puppy outside, digging up the flowers,
it's warm, jumping legs and my cold knees.

I feel my warm duvet, touching my rough feet
and the soft carpet as I walk.

I smell hot, jammy toast and sit on the sofa,
crunching my breakfast.

I hear my mum's shouts and we all leave just
in time for school.

**Raffles Moulder (10)**
**St David's Primary School, Moreton-in-Marsh**

## Horror

An overblown lampshade rammed in my face
get out of bed and see my school clothes
reminding me of doom.
Go to breakfast, the best thing in the world,
drink my cup of tea and fill my bag, thinking
of the hell I've got to go to.
Walking to school, seeing most of my mates
on the way.

Go past the witch-like figures around the church,
looking at the ground that I will one day be in.
See Jack Frost looking for his next victim,
get to the gates, it looks like a jail,
I walk in and up to the top playground
to play on the ice.
But then, the horror rings, we have to approach
the school to our desks,
All of the blinds covering the windows like bars,
all of our desks are empty.
Oh no, we start the lesson.

**Gary Luker (11)**
St David's Primary School, Moreton-in-Marsh


## My Journey To School

Listen . . . I hear whistling wind swirling
Listen . . . I hear children shouting in the playground
Listen . . . I hear footsteps crunching on the crispy leaves
Listen . . . I hear cars spluttering across the road.

Look . . . I see frost covered grass, shimmering like a
                                  thousand diamonds
Look . . . I see skeletal leaves falling to the ground
Look . . . I see children sliding on iced glass covered earth.
Look . . . I see glistening cars shining in the sun.

Stop . . . I smell the fresh air starting a new day.

**Zara Oliver (11)**
St David's Primary School, Moreton-in-Marsh

# Going To School

I wake up and some arms stretch like a tiger,
I see my mum stamping like an elephant,
My wardrobe is like a monster going to eat me
And a hawk that just lies there still as can be.
I hear my dog barking, *Let me out!*
Some birds are singing like a choir and my sister,
Sounding like a bee buzzing in my room.
I feel a sweet rosy kiss from my mum and
My slippers are like a hot water bottle as
I walk downstairs.

I go into the sitting room,
Waiting to feel the horror, my sister, argue with me.
I see Weetabix shaped like a boat floating on a sea of fresh milk.
Then I get in the car, shivering and unhappy that I'm going to school.

Then the engine starts, like we're in a race,
I go and give my friend a lift as I walk on her grass
It's like cornflakes crunching under my feet.
Then we're near the gate, we go through the gates
And shout, 'We're here, the work starts here!'

**Catriona Wilcox (9)**
St David's Primary School, Moreton-in-Marsh


# Going To School

I hear the sound of my mum waking up,
the squeaking of my metal stairs and bedroom door
the waterfall shower and clanking of dishes.
My sister getting told again and again, to hurry.

I feel the cold laminate flooring on my feet,
the warm rug, half-opened eyes blurred to the world,
a slow smile as I meet my cat.

I clamber onto the sofa, put on my shoes
and rush to the car. We're off!
Into the playground, the bell rings.

**Jessica Ashby (9)**
St David's Primary School, Moreton-in-Marsh

## Going To School

I wake up to the sound of a purring mass of black fur
I wake up, check for snow, I can't see anything, my eyes are a blur
I wake up, shove on clothes and hurry down the stairs
I wake up, see a whining, stinky lap-dog, his feet are all in pairs.

In my breakfast of Shredded Wheat, one floating like a raft
In my breakfast, I've never seen something quite so daft
My breakfast has been finished, now I pack my lunch
My breakfast has been good, I like the way I eat, because
                                                    it goes crunch.

In the bathroom, I approach the buzzing bristles, put on toothpaste
                                                    and brush
In the bathroom, as I wash my brush, the water comes out suddenly
                                                    in one fast rush
In the bathroom, looking around I see in the fish tank, a little bridge
In the bathroom, listening I hear chinking milk bottles as my dad
                                                    opens the fridge.

On my way to school, icicles stuck fast
On my way to school, walking on the path, pondering on the past
I arrive at school, oh great!

**Alex Rycroft (9)**
St David's Primary School, Moreton-in-Marsh


## My Journey To School

Listen . . . I hear the whistling wind, heading north
Listen . . . I hear children shouting, breaking ice on puddles
Listen . . . I hear cars spluttering to a slow start
Listen . . . I hear footsteps crunching on the icy grass.

Look . . . I see sparkling crystals melting into ice droplets
Look . . . I see a field, a white sheet glinting as I zoomed by
Look . . . I see a sunrise, a strawberry milkshake floating into the sky.
Look . . . I see icy windows inside of the car as I look around.

**Bethany Bowles Moore (10)**
St David's Primary School, Moreton-in-Marsh

## Going To School

I hear the thundering voice of my dad, the
moaning of my sister, people on the stairs,
creaking floorboards.

I enter the capital of food and drink, the giant
slobber-chops is on the floor, snoring a silent
tune to herself. I get my breakfast and hear the
crunch, crunch of cereal in my mouth.

I go upstairs, put my music on, get dressed
and hear the rustle of fingers on the window.
I brush my teeth and wash my face with
wishy, woshy water.

I go downstairs, pack my bag and off I go,
I see my friends. The dread of the day awaits
as the school bell rings.

**Joshua Kelly (10)**
St David's Primary School, Moreton-in-Marsh


## My Journey

Shh . . . I hear the cars zooming down the motorway
Shh . . . I hear the crashing waves
Shh . . . I hear children laughing
Shh . . . I hear the wailing of the arcade.

Look . . . I see surfers riding the waves
Look . . . I see children playing in the park
Look . . . I see cars zooming across the motorway
Look . . . I see the crystal sky.

Umm . . . I smell the fish and chips
Umm . . . I smell the salty sea
Umm . . . I smell the swimming pool
Umm . . . I smell the ice cream van.

**Michael Creed (9)**
St David's Primary School, Moreton-in-Marsh

## The Jab

Today's the day, the dreaded day that we go to the nurse,
'Get in the car and put your belt on,'
Says my dad, as he puts the car into reverse.
The engine starts with a thundering splutter
And off we drive to the nurse.
The journey seems to last for a lifetime,
We slowly climb out of the Rover.
We slink through the door
Knees a-shaking,
The clinicy smell that our noses intake.
We knock on the door, the nurse awaits
Needle in hand, ready to kill.
I sit in the chair shaking all over,
The nurse gets closer, kneels by my side.
'This won't hurt a bit,' she says, getting ready.
She plunges it in . . .
It's over already!

**Peter Rycroft (11)**
**St David's Primary School, Moreton-in-Marsh**


## Going To School

Wakey, wakey, sleepy head!
My room, as black as midnight.
I hear cats purring, dogs barking.
Breakfast waiting to be eaten.
Feeling chilly air frosty, wind rushing around,
Getting dressed, feeling sleepy.
Tired eyes, yawning, stretching, washing face,
Cleaning teeth, brushing hair.
Pack my lunch into my bag, coat on, shoes buckled.
Frost shines and glistens on the windows of the car.
Climb in, fasten my belt.
I'm ready for my journey to school.

**Claire Bartlet (11)**
**St David's Primary School, Moreton-in-Marsh**

## A Journey To The Operation Room

Ouch . . . I feel the pain in my left leg,
As I zoom through corridors,
Ugh . . . I smell the scent of medicines,
I can feel my heart beating inside my chest,
Bursting to come out.

Shh . . . I hear the nurses discussing my leg,
As I whoosh round the corner,
I would have so much preferred to stay and listen
Argh . . . I see the doctors and the nurses peering over me,
Mum! Dad! I hear me scream inside my head.

I see the doors getting closer,
Suddenly, I burst through them.
Big bold letters on the door saying, Operation Room
I fly through the doors into the room
It's their turn now!

**Chloe White (10)**
St David's Primary School, Moreton-in-Marsh


## The Journey

Shh . . . I hear the fresh rustling of the trees swaying
in the morning wind
Shh . . . I hear the birds singing their wake-up song
Shh . . . I hear cars speeding down the road to their destination.

Look . . . I see people in a mad rush
Look . . . I see grass where Jack Frost has visited overnight
I hear the ground crunch as I move over it.

Hmm . . . I smell a full English that no one could resist
Hmm . . . I smell fresh air that no cars could pollute
Hmm . . . I smell deodorant from people who pass me by.

Shh . . . What can *you* hear?

**Jack Davey (10)**
St David's Primary School, Moreton-in-Marsh

## My Journey To School

Shh . . . I hear the scraping of the ice,
The rustling of cold and wet trees,
The crunching of the grass,
And the tweeting of a bright red robin.

Look . . . I see the flowing of a river,
A dull grey squirrel jumping from tree to tree,
An acorn in its mouth.

Shh . . . I hear the calling of a little boy,
The engine of a jumbled car,
The opening of a squeaky door,
The hooting of a car horn, bidding farewell.

Look . . . I see the frozen school gate,
Boys skidding on the ice,
The girls bounding together to gossip.

Umm . . . I smell the sweet scent of flowers in the class,
The fresh air falling through the window,
The bitter smell of work heading towards me.

**Chris Arthurs (9)**
**St David's Primary School, Moreton-in-Marsh**


## Journey

Listen . . .
Shh . . . I hear whistling wind heading north.
Shh . . . I hear footsteps on the crunchy grass.
Shh . . . I hear children's laughter in the playground.
Shh . . . I hear cars spluttering along the road.

Wait . . .
Look . . . I see a blood-red sunset, beginning the day.
Look . . . I see snow falling upon the treetops.
Look . . . I see cloudy skies in the midnight moon.
Look . . . I see frost on the grass shining like diamonds.

**Lauren Griffin (10)**
**St David's Primary School, Moreton-in-Marsh**

## The Journey

Look . . . I see the ice-white Earth, like a million shards of glass.
Look . . . I see the frosty grass, gleaming in the sunlight.
Look . . . I see the sun - a golden disc floating through the misty sky.

Shh . . . I hear the crunch of a twig that someone trod on.
Shh . . . I hear the tweeting of birds gliding amongst the treetops.
Shh . . . I hear the clatter of a horse, trotting past.

Mmm . . . I smell the scent of wild flowers under my feet.
Mmm . . . I smell the evergreen trees in the far distance.
Mmm . . . I smell the fresh sandwiches in the picnic hamper.

**Paige Amber Snuggs (11)**
St David's Primary School, Moreton-in-Marsh

## The Journey

Doors opening
Engines roaring
Wheels spinning on glittering ice.

Rain hitting
Sun rising
A rainbow appearing in the distance.

An open window
Rivers rushing
Fish drifting in the current.

A plane passing
Birds singing
Wind howling, bushes rustling.

The trees swaying
Sun fading
Moon appearing
Stars shining
We're slowly drifting, drifting off to sleep.

**Tom Barry (10)**
St David's Primary School, Moreton-in-Marsh

## My Journey

Shh . . . I hear branches dropping to the ground
Shh . . . I hear creaking twigs underfoot
Shh . . . I hear people plodding closer and closer
Shh . . . I hear thunder coming this way.

Umm . . . I smell an odour in the mist
Umm . . . I smell trouble out there
Umm . . . I smell dust out in the distance
Umm . . . I smell bones rotting in a graveyard.

Oh I see people riding bikes,
Oh I see houses being created.
Oh I see future cars being made,
Oh I see my house in the country.

Hmm . . . I feel wood around me,
Hmm . . . I feel waters goodness.
Hmm . . . I feel the window's freshness,
Hmm . . . I feel fresh air pushing past me.

**Connor McQueen (9) & William Jacka (10)**
St David's Primary School, Moreton-in-Marsh


## Going To School

When I wake up I feel a wet nose rubbing my cheeks,
like a snail crawling on me.
I sit up slowly, still half asleep and walk over to where
my clothes were left the previous night.

The bathroom is empty, no sign of life.
My toothbrush stares at me with its two eyes either side
of the handle and its brush like a prickly white feather duster.

At the kitchen table, I hear the whistle of the kettle go,
it sounds like children screaming at the top of their voices.

**Chelsea Clapperton (11)**
St David's Primary School, Moreton-in-Marsh

## Journey To The Beach

Flip-flop, flip-flop, begins children's flip-flops
Lots of people in short tops
Umm yum, fish and chips
Lots of people lick their lips

Here comes the ice cream van
There are lots of people getting a tan
Blow up boats
And rubber floats

Children building in the sand
Children darting on the land
Adults cycling on their bikes
Babies playing games they like

Children playing in the sea
Adults having cups of tea
Children in the rock pools
I can hear the lifeguard's calls

Adults play the ball game cricket
People paying for car park tickets
People inflating
People skating

It's getting dark
There's no one in the park
I don't want to go into the porch
Holding the torch.

**Emily White (10)**
St David's Primary School, Moreton-in-Marsh

# Journey Home

*Home!*
I'm going, I know,
To hear, to see, to smell,
Listen to me, now I tell.

I can hear car engines,
Rattling of tins,
I can hear the mewing of cats,
Barking of dogs,
Turning of taps,
Rolling of logs,

*Home!*
I can smell the cooking of cakes,
Water in lakes.
I can smell flowers' odour,
Strong perfume
The smell of soda.
Car fumes.

*Home!*
I can see an icy lake,
A woman just about to bake.
I can see the moon so bright,
Like a rainy puddle,
I can see a welcoming light,
I'm waiting for my cuddle.
I'm *home!*

**Bethan Wookey (9)**
**St David's Primary School, Moreton-in-Marsh**

# Journey Through The Seasons

In winter on my journey I see . . .
Powdery snow covering ground.
I see . . .
People slipping and sliding on ice.
I see . . .
Shades of blue and white covering land.
I see . . .
Jack Frost has worked his magic,
I feel . . .
A cold breeze down my back.

In spring on my journey I see . . .
Buds starting to flower.
I see . . .
Birds making nests from twigs,
I see . . .
Blossom of pink, yellow and white.
I see . . .
Fluffy baby chicks are born.
I see . . .
Lambs leaping across fields.

In summer on my journey I see . . .
Green leaves filling the trees
I see . . .
The hot sun blazing in the sky.
I see . . .
Flowers fill fields and gardens,
I see . . .
Children splashing each other in paddling pools.
I see . . .
Families enjoying holidays of fun and days at the beach.

In the autumn on my journey I see . . .
Brown leaves scattered everywhere,
I feel . . .
Weather getting slightly colder.
I see . . .
Trees losing their leaves.
I see . . .
Everywhere covered in reds, oranges and browns.
I see . . .
Plants are sleeping.

**Rhiannon Williams (10)**
St David's Primary School, Moreton-in-Marsh

## A Journey On A Summer's Day

Long snaking roads,
Small trees flashing by.
The sun, a ball of fire,
Floating in the sky.

Cows mooing loudly,
Calves sleeping near.
Rabbits in the hedgerow,
With several little deer.

The sky a diamond blue,
As clear as any glass.
Birds soaring high,
Going very fast.

Trees large and green,
Flowers standing tall.
Horses big and proud,
Ponies really small!

Spreading out before me
The land lay beautiful.

**Emma Chaning-Pearce (11)**
St David's Primary School, Moreton-in-Marsh

## Journey

Walking through the country
I can see
A frozen lake
The first bumblebee.

Walking through the country
I can smell
The sweet scent of snowdrops
Crisp fresh air.

Walking through the country
I can see
Silver frost
Brown gnarled trees.

Walking through the country
I can hear
The enchanting sound of songbirds
The rustling of trees.

Walking through the country
I can't see
Getting dark now
Let's go home.

**Lucy Speechley (9)**
St David's Primary School, Moreton-in-Marsh

## My Journey To School

Look, a red sea of sweatshirts
Breathe the pink odour of a rose,
Look, a blue lake of the sky,
Look ,a white cotton street of snow.
Breathe the green smell of fresh grass in the air.
Look, a yellow shine of the sun,
Look, a brown thickness of the mud.
Look, a black darkness of the night sky,
Look, a grey glumness of the mist.

**Alice Fowler (10)**
St David's Primary School, Moreton-in-Marsh

## Journey To School

On the way to school
I felt the ice outside the door,
It's like stepping into a huge freezer.

The sound of the cars rushing by
As I walk to school.

The sound of the train like water
Rushing down a waterfall.

The feel of the warmth when I step into school
Like falling to sleep in bed.

The sound of the clock
Ticking in class.

The feel of the bread when we're eating
At lunchtime.

The sound of people talking
On our way home.

**Nicole Holden (11)**
**St David's Primary School, Moreton-in-Marsh**


## Journey To My Cousin's House

The wind, cold as ice,
The snow, falling like white rain
But just as fast.
Teeth are chattering like hail
On glass.
The sound of children playing
Like a carnival in the past.
The snow as white as paper,
Footprints in the snow.
Snow everywhere you look,
Some on my toe,
I like snow as much as you do
But the next day, it was gone.

**Hollie Teagle (9)**
**St David's Primary School, Moreton-in-Marsh**

# Going To School

*Waking up*
When I wake up I look out of my window and I can see the
white frosty grass and the people walking by. I can see my clothes
on the floor by my bed and I can hear my mum and dad talking and
they are listening to the loud radio and I'm feeling happy.

*Breakfast*
I come downstairs and I smell bacon on toast which my mum
is cooking for my dad. My brother asks for some, but my mum
shouts at him very loudly. I hear the door slam as my dad
goes off to work.

*Bathroom*
I go into the bathroom and get my brush and start brushing
my hair to make it straight. After I brush my teeth, I go to my mum
and say hello to her and then I go and see my brother.

*Living Room*
I go in and put the television on and watch for about half an hour
and then my mum puts my bag down where I'm sitting and I wait
until it's time to go.

*Friends*
When I get to school, I meet my friends and we talk until the bell goes
but before that people give in their letters everybody rushes in and
I can hear the sound of feet clumping up the stairs and they are
very noisy.

**Chelsie Scarrott (9)**
St David's Primary School, Moreton-in-Marsh


# Seasons

In autumn, leaves fall swirling, swiftly, silently,
In winter there's frost, freezing cold.
In summer there's sun, hot, hot, boiling hot.
In spring there's boughs of white, white snowy blossom.

**Sally Keeley (9) & Alistair Swift (11)**
St David's Primary School, Moreton-in-Marsh

# Going To School

*Waking up*
I hear the avalanche of my dad's voice telling me to, 'Get up!'
The bark of my dog, waking me.
The cars passing by my window,
I see the cold bedroom floor,
The fluffy steps,
I feel the freezing cold banister,
The warm fluffy carpet.

*Breakfast*
I hear the sound of the TV blasting in,
The sounds of spoon on the bowls.
I see the cold breeze swaying the bush
The packed lunch
I felt the metal spoons
The cold milky bowl.

*Getting ready*
I hear the shower dripping
I see the taps running,
The cold shower curtain,
I feel the cold black plug,
The warm towel.

*Going . . .*
I go downstairs
I hear my dad packing my lunch
The sound of bags being opened
I see the hair brush
The paint of our walls
I feel the warm settee
The stony fireplace.

**Lily Taylor (10)**
St David's Primary School, Moreton-in-Marsh

## Going To School

*Waking up:*
I see my television buzzing like a bee, people staring.
Shadows like statues on my wall.
Trains roaring on the track, cars slowly driving,
Mum snoring like a hippo.
The smell of fresh fragrant air,
The sweet smell of breakfast,
The smell of radiators, burning.

*In the bathroom:*
A wide eyed person staring, a tub as big as my bed.
A heat-seeker, burning wildly,
The doom of the toilet flushing.
The gurgling of the water when I clean my teeth.

*Getting dressed:*
I tumble down the dreaded stairs.
The worry of the dreaded school uniform.
The horror of the school.

*My walk to school:*
The dread of what awaits me in my quest to conquer
The dreaded school day.

**Jodie Walker (9)**
St David's Primary School, Moreton-in-Marsh


## On The Way To School

I hear cars speeding past like lightning,
Cold children stamping their feet
Like thunder rocking the sky.
I hear the water flowing like a twisted snake,
Slithering through the grass.
The baby sheep like fluffy clouds,
Lorries beeping their horns and
The sun shining, like a ball of fire.

**Luke Davis (11)**
St David's Primary School, Moreton-in-Marsh

# Going To School

*Bathroom*
Waking up, hearing fast cars rushing to get to work,
like younger children on bumper cars at the funfair.
Seeing a straw wash basket, animals pick at it and eat it.
Feeling like it's a dark bat cave, just waiting to scare me.

*Hallway*
Waking up, hearing the heating going on,
I get shivers up my bony spine.
Seeing long closed-in walls, there are delicate bedrooms,
I'm in a wonderland.
Feeling a red long silky carpet with falling roses,
Just waiting for Oscars to be won.
A top class model walking the catwalk, wearing thousands
of sassy designer clothes, looking a million dollars.

*Kitchen*
Waking up, hearing bowls and doors closing, *clonk*.
Feeling like I'm on a hot, faraway island with palm trees.
Seeing joyful happy faces, ready to greet me.
Smelling the fresh milk, straight from the fridge,
The porridge, lumpy like mud.

**Elizabeth Coley (10)**
**St David's Primary School, Moreton-in-Marsh**


# The Journey

The whistling of the old oak trees,
The dropping of rain like falling icicles.
The beep, beep, beep of the crossing
Like a warning of danger.

The black BMW, like a silent panther.
A dark face looking out of the window said he
Was my mum's friend, let me in the black leathery car.
Drove me away and never brought me back!

**James Lucking (10)**
**St David's Primary School, Moreton-in-Marsh**

## Outside

Walking outside I hear the sound of teeth clanging together
as my friends build icy snowmen. I see crispy leaves covered in ice.
Pawprints into the snow from my cats.

Wandering to the kitchen smelling my mum baking cakes
and cookies on the stove for my family.
Smelling my uncle lighting a fire in the living room.

Watching the garden, seeing birds making prints in the snow
and mother birds feeding their babies in the distance.
I see a woodpecker feeding his family as well.

**Amy McCauley (10)**
St David's Primary School, Moreton-in-Marsh


## Going To School

*Waking up*
Rubbing my eyes and realising it's morning
Looking out of the window, the man in the moon looking at me
The sound of the dripping tap, drip drop, drip drop
Dad showering, getting ready for work
The school uniform waiting to be put on.

*Breakfast*
A biscuit and a drink ready for me
The family sitting round the table, eating breakfast
The slurping of my mum, drinking coffee, slurp slurp
The banging of the back door as my sister goes
To catch the bus for school.

*Walk to school*
The rustling leaves of the old trees
Cars rushing past on their tired way to work
Clip clop, clip clop go my weary feet
Hitting the damp pavement
Finally I see it, the school.

**Charlotte Jeffs (10)**
St David's Primary School, Moreton-in-Marsh

## Going To School

*Waking up*
A bright light like a sunbeam.
My brother crying like nails down a chalk board.
Everything looks fuzzy from just waking up.

*Bathroom*
Falling out of bed like falling off the top of Mount Everest,
Hearing the showers turning on, it's like torture.

*Getting dressed*
I feel the cold school clothes on my warm skin
Like ice in boiling water.

*Breakfast*
I walk down the windy staircase to the breakfast table,
Where smells of all sorts greet me, but I'm not eating much.

**Jessica Crockett (10)**
St David's Primary School, Moreton-in-Marsh


## On The Way To School

On the way to school one day
Leaves like crispy crisps crumble
As cold as Jack Frost
The sun was coming out as hot as chilli, red-hot
Trains flashing by like police sirens
Ice on the floor
As hard as iron
People rushing by cars on a main road
Water like rushing bulls after red rags.

I hear children running to school
Like a herd of animals
The school bell rings
Like a headache banging in my head
That's what I hear on the way to school.

**Brandon J Lawley (10)**
St David's Primary School, Moreton-in-Marsh

## Journey To . . . ?

Cars go past like thunder, not aware of children,
The tears of the rain, sensing sadness,
Trees shedding their small brown skin,
Graves crumbling from the harsh cold,
Flowers dying like a death blanket's covered them,
Solitary black cars with the large wooden coffin,
People weeping like leaking pipes,
This happened as I watched from the top.

The bus moved on to a long street,
I could see on my right, a girl and her father
Shouting spite.
Slamming doors and china smashing,
The drum roll of the stairs,
Crying from the window,
Shouting in the lounge.
Emerging gorilla-like man in a denim jacket,
Leaving the house towards the pub.

**Suzanna Tyack (11)**
**St David's Primary School, Moreton-in-Marsh**


## Journey To School

I quickly walk down the main road
Over the bulging bridge
I see trains
Slithering along the railway line
Like a long snake
I walk further
Feeling the cool air blowing against me
Like a cold freezer door being opened
Then I stop
I hear rustling leaves
Twirling round on the floor
Like a speeding hurricane.

**Demi Davies (9)**
**St David's Primary School, Moreton-in-Marsh**

## Going To School

*My bedroom*
Opening my sleepy eyes, my room is pitch-black
The ringing of my alarm wakes me,
Stepping to my window, pulling back the curtain
To the dark, shadowy houses and the street lamps
Are all lost in the mist.

*Downstairs*
Plodding down, the wind whistling through the keyhole,
Hearing purring, rushing in the kitchen 'pop'
Toast's done, spreading with melty butter.

*Bathroom*
Blinds clattering, a cold damp,
Slippery tiles, dark and gloomy.
Freezing water trickles down my body.

*On the way to school*
Walk down a pebble path through a creaky gate,
Seeing cars rushing by, beeping in rage.
Flowers blooming in the sunlight as the day has
Only just begun.

**Lauren Baldwyn (10)**
**St David's Primary School, Moreton-in-Marsh**


## Journey Poem

Last leaf was about to fall,
Ice was as cold as snow.
Cars were stuck in the traffic lights
Until the sign said, *Go!*

Sun was getting very high,
Up, up in the sky.
Sun like a ball of fire,
Still higher and higher.

I heard a bus set off from its stop,
It started up with a big loud pop.

**Andrew Coyne (9)**
**St David's Primary School, Moreton-in-Marsh**

## Going To School

*I wake up*
I see a blue and white pillow with a head mark in the middle,
A fat stupid ball of fluff, blending in with my rug.
A quiet but annoying voice, telling me to wake up, repeatedly.
A bunch of grey poles hurting my feet.
I see a drawer full of clothes, picking out my uniform.
I hear the rustle of my T-shirt as I put it over my head.
I see a bunch of mountains waiting to be climbed down,
I see a hot steamy plate of toast and tea and a dog begging
at my feet.

I hear my mum shouting, 'The bus is here!'
A rush for my school shoes, sometimes I fail,
As I walk out, a blast of frost hits me like a train.
I walk up the bus steps and place myself at the back.
A conversation goes on about school and social life,
I look out of the window. It's a blur of cars and trees,
The bus stops eventually. I walk off and I'm at school.

**Ben Croft (10)**
**St David's Primary School, Moreton-in-Marsh**


## Monday Morning

I wake to a delicious smell of breakfast,
tempting me down the stairs,
I see my brother watching cartoons
as I sit down on a chair.
The toaster pops as the toast pops out,
the milk makes my Krispies crunch.
My brother comes to chew on his toast
as I enjoy a munch.
My mum gives me grief
so I go upstairs and brush my teeth.
My dad calls me down, 'It's time to go,'
I put my shoes on, but my brother shouts, 'No.'
And we are off.

**Jack Oughton (10)**
**St David's Primary School, Moreton-in-Marsh**

## Going To School

Waking up in my room I hear the roar of the shower,
and the loud noise of the cars speeding past.
My brother's alarm clock getting him up
to catch the school bus.
Walking to the window, I see my big garden
and all the fruit trees and wild bushes blowing
in the wind.
My dogs running around with each other.

Wandering to the kitchen, I smell the fresh milk
just come out of the fridge.
I wander to the other end of the kitchen,
bend down and get my bowl.
I fill it with cereal, it floats around like a
lost fish in the sea.

**George Wright (10)**
St David's Primary School, Moreton-in-Marsh


## Journey To The School

The wind howling like a dog,
Motor cars rumbling like thunder,
The rain hitting the car
As hard as rocks.

The frost, white as icing,
The roads as slippery as snakes,
Children crying like cold kittens,
The grass, sparkling like glitter.

The gloomy dark sky,
Full of black clouds.
The cold air freezing you,
That's what it feels like
On my journey to school.

**Ellie Marie Marshall (9)**
St David's Primary School, Moreton-in-Marsh

## Are We There Yet?

Going on holiday,
Sitting in the car,
*Are we there yet?*

We're going camping,
Lots and lots to see,
*Are we there yet?*

It's hot at the beach,
Warmer than home,
*Are we there yet?*

Staying in a tent,
Though I miss my comfy bed!
*Are we there yet?*

Nearly there, I'm sure,
Who can see the sea?
*Are we there yet?*

Yes, yes, yes!
Whoopee, whoopee, whoopee
*We're there!*

**Sarah Thompson (9)**
St David's Primary School, Moreton-in-Marsh

## A Journey To School

I walk to school
On a cold, frosty morning,
Falling over wood that splinters fast.
It starts to snow,
Mint, white flakes like icicles,
And hail hits the ground,
Smashing into tiny crystals.

**Martin Bateman (10)**
St David's Primary School, Moreton-in-Marsh

## Going To School

*Waking up:*
I wake up and see the bright light, like a sunbeam,
I toss and turn like there are ants all over me.

*In the bathroom:*
I trudge along to the sink and pick up my blue icicle
Toothbrush, lift my toothpaste and brush my gappy teeth.

*Getting dressed:*
I crawl to the undesirable school uniform and pull it on me.

*Breakfast:*
I trail downstairs and see my brother and sister watching TV.
I walk to the kitchen, still only half awake.
The kitchen is a cream colour with new units and a fridge.
I make my breakfast, sit down and relax.

*Getting ready:*
I now rush around getting my shoes on,
Brushing my hair and collecting my homework.

*Going to school:*
I wait in the bus stop, freezing cold.
Waiting, waiting, waiting. The bus comes, I go to school
I get to school, my friends rush to greet me.

**Victoria Firth (10)**
St David's Primary School, Moreton-in-Marsh


## My Journey Of Colour

Red . . . a flock of bright sweatshirts,
Pink . . . the rose of the sunset,
Blue . . . the lake of the sky,
White . . . the cotton wool of the snow,
Green . . . the gleam of the grass,
Yellow . . . the shimmering of the sun,
Brown . . . the foulness of the mud,
Black . . . the darkness of the night sky,
Grey . . . the glumness of the mist.

**Megan Jarvis (9)**
St David's Primary School, Moreton-in-Marsh

## Going To School

I find light pouring from my window,
and the shower is still dripping.
The warm duvet on top of me
but I still get up.

The spiky pricks of my toothbrush
scraping my teeth,
The fresh smell of air freshener
going up my nostrils.

The feel of the cat rubbing my legs
for more food.
The sound of the sprinkle of the
cereal as I pour
Then the TV is turned up to an
ear-piercing sound.

I hear the rustling of the trees,
scattering its leaves.
Jack Frost's breath trying to freeze me,
and the noise of the bus as it opens
its frosty doors to welcome me.

**Rachel Firth (10)**
**St David's Primary School, Moreton-in-Marsh**


## Going To School

I wake to an earthquake through the wall
and fall down the rickety bunk bed ladder.
I stagger to the bathroom and later hear the
monster's roar of the toilet flushing.
I walk back into my bedroom and hear a skeleton creak.
I spin round to find it's my brother yawning.
I get changed and slide down the mountain of the stairs.
I quickly scoff my hot toast and drink my hot, sweet tea.
Finally, at 8.30 I set off, I see friends and enemies
Before I pass through the gates of doom.

**Liam Annakin (11)**
**St David's Primary School, Moreton-in-Marsh**

# Going To School

*Waking up*
Big brindle, ball of fluff, licking me round the face,
the trickle of water in the sink, splashing and sploshing
in the grey, dull sink.
Sound of cars travelling on the road.

*Bathroom*
A clunk sound of when I lower the plug into the dark hole
that leads to a smelly drain,
A trickle as the sink fills and it splashes the light blue walls.
The noise downstairs is my mum shouting at my dad
to help make breakfast.

*Getting dressed*
As I put on my clothes and look out of the window,
and see the frost that greets me on the doorstep.
My mum tells me to hurry as I look out through my window.

*Breakfast*
The buttery taste on my slightly brown toast
and the sweetness of my cold, soft and fruity drink.

**Sophie Halley (9)**
**St David's Primary School, Moreton-in-Marsh**


# Journey To School

On my way to school,
Seeing rushing people
Like squirrels collecting nuts,
Clouds, like fluffy woolly jumpers,
Market as busy as a beehive,
Shouting of desperate market sellers,
Continual beep, beep of the crossing,
Cold air blowing away like a balloon,
Stinging touch of frost.

**Sophie Marshall (9)**
**St David's Primary School, Moreton-in-Marsh**

## Journey To School In Winter

The wind howling like a wolf,
Flakes of snow twisting and turning.
Teeth chatter and clatter,
Skidding cars braking fast.
Now cars crashing loudly,
*Crash! Crash!*
Children's faces, pale as snow,
Keeping warm, wrapped against the cold.
The snow as white as new paper,
But colder than a freezer.
Car motors rumbling like thunder,
I feel the frostbite on my toes.
Shivering like an earthquake
I enter the school,
*Warm at last!*

**Rosie Clark (9) & Emily Sullivan (10)**
St David's Primary School, Moreton-in-Marsh


## Journey Poem

Last leaf was about to fall,
Frost was as cold as snow,
Cars were stuck in traffic lights
Until the sign said *Go!*

Sun was getting very high,
Up and up in the sky.
Sun was like a ball of fire,
Still climbing higher, higher.

I heard a bus set off from its stop,
It started up with a big, loud pop!

**James Stansbury (9)**
St David's Primary School, Moreton-in-Marsh

## The Journey

Shh: I hear the waving trees on the frosty morning.
Shh: I hear the tweeting birds on the frosty morning.
Shh: I hear the loud children on the frosty morning.
Shh: I hear the ice breaking on the frosty morning.

Look: I see the busy traffic on the icy morning.
Look: I see the barking dog on the icy morning.
Look: I see the purring cat on the icy morning.
Look: I see the chattering people on the icy morning.

Umm: I smell the fresh air on the summer's day.
Umm: I smell the oily engines on the summer's day.
Umm: I smell the pretty flowers on the summer's day.
Umm: I smell the bee's honey on the summer's day.

**Gaby Shakespeare (11)**
**St David's Primary School, Moreton-in-Marsh**


## Going To School

I wake up in the morning,
I see a boiling hot ball of fire in the sky,
I see myself in the mirror,
I see cars going by.

I walk to my bathroom,
I hear my cat purring at the window.

Wandering to school,
I feel cold and tired,
But my feet break down
And I stand still looking around.

**Callum Gibson (9)**
**St David's Primary School, Moreton-in-Marsh**

## Journey To School

You step outside,
The cold air hits your face,
Like wind at full blast.
Ice on the step,
Ice on the path like you're on an ice rink.
Coldness on your bottom
When you slip over.

The train pulling out
Of the station,
Like whippets going after rabbits.
The train driver waves or beeps his horn.

Pressing the traffic light,
All of a sudden, *beep, beep, beep,*
Like an annoying alarm clock.
Walk into school,
The heating is like a blanket.

**Kitty Teague (11)**
St David's Primary School, Moreton-in-Marsh


## Journey From School

Sun setting earlier each day,
Leaves crunching,
Cosmic cars zooming
As fast as fireworks.
Wind growing up,
Not as many people outside.
Autumn's breeze fades,
Autumn fades away,
We all huddle up,
Like hibernating squirrels.

**Timothy Swatman Allen (9)**
St David's Primary School, Moreton-in-Marsh

## The Journey To Death!

The click of a bike changing gear,
Ice crunching like mini earthquakes,
Sweat dripping like faraway streams,
Roads as steep as mountains high,
A heart beating like a big bass drum,
The screech of a car suddenly stopping,
Footsteps were so slow and steady,
A cold hand like ice grabbing an unsuspecting face,
Words echo as hollow as a cave,
Neck rope like a snake squeezing its prey,
Blood as red as a poppy,
The boot of a car, dark as a demon's lair,
The glimmer of a knife like the sun on the sea,
The pleas of a child to let them go free.

**Keira-Mae Ladbrook (11)**
St David's Primary School, Moreton-in-Marsh


## Journey To School

My squeaky little brother shouting,
The car thundering down the road.
People shouting, rushing past,
The leaves full of white snow.

Then I stepped out of the car,
The cold breeze brushing against my face,
Other cars rushing past me on the dusty road.

As soon as I step into school,
The heat is like a hot water bottle.

**Sam Dyer (9)**
St David's Primary School, Moreton-in-Marsh

# Hunter

A flash of orange stripes
Whizzing past the trees.
Panting breath, cracking twigs,
A scent smelt on the breeze.

A gentle creature resting,
Lapping at a stream.
The seeker spots his prey,
The victim has been seen.

He waits, the tension mounting,
His patience wearing thin.
He eyes his prey, prepares to pounce,
This reward he needs to win.

A twig cracks underfoot,
The tiger hears a grunting.
A rustling in the darkness,
He's not the only one who's hunting.

Tiger hears a distant clicking,
The aiming of a gun.
He smells the fear of another,
A shot - the tiger's gone.

We are the real hunters.

**Francesca Gardner (11)**
St Lawrence CE Primary School, Lechlade


# Nature

N is for nut trees growing in the background,
A is for angler fish, in the reefs it swims around,
T is for turtle, deep down in the sea,
U is for umbrella bird, in the sky it wants to be,
R is for rabbit that enjoys a dig,
E is for elephant, so heavy and so big.

**Lawrence Gammond (11)**
St Lawrence CE Primary School, Lechlade

## Wildlife Walk

Soaring high,
High in the sky,
An eagle hunts its prey.
It spots some movement down below,
And dives to where it lays.

A falcon scanning the canyon's face
Spots its prey and pursues with grace.
A chinchilla rat darts from beneath a rock,
It sees the falcon and squats with shock.

A tiger roaming the African plains
Pounces on its prey and strikes, and gains.
It tears the flesh and rips the skin,
The blood is dripping from his chin.

A lion resting in the shade of a tree,
He raises his head and what does he see?
A herd of buffalo charging past,
They're trampling everything, they're going too fast!

**Charlotte Hall (11)**
St Lawrence CE Primary School, Lechlade


## Wildlife

W ind and water, air and land,
 I think of these as I travel around.
 L ife is everywhere, all you have to do is stand and stare.
 D ragonflies dart around, a quiet buzzing is their sound,
 L izards and reptiles like the sun.
 I bis are sacred birds of Egypt.
 F ish are gentle things, but some fish are vicious killers.
 E agles dive down on prey and tear it apart, and eat all day.

**Jack Bestwick (10)**
St Lawrence CE Primary School, Lechlade

## Three Little Candles

There were three little candles sitting in a hold,
Two had been lit, but one was still bold.
The little one said, 'Why can't I be lit like you older folk?'
And the other two said, 'You're too young to smoke.'

The little one went hot and started to melt,
Nobody knew how he felt.
First there was a spark, then he lit,
They were all shocked and thought they had nits.

There were three little candles sitting in their hold,
Three were lit, but none were bold.

**Benjamin Woodard (10)**
St Lawrence CE Primary School, Lechlade


## Animals

Which animal do you like the best?
At night, cats and dogs are quite a pest.
Strays running through the street,
An injured dog you might just meet.

Cows plodding to the river,
During the winter months the cows shiver.
Shetland ponies in the field,
Hopefully the gate is sealed.

Koalas in the trees,
Bushbabies in the day lie sleepily,
Kangaroos bouncing their hearts out,
Cheetahs are the fastest, without a doubt.

**Conrad Nuttall (10)**
St Lawrence CE Primary School, Lechlade

## Wildlife

Trees shudder in the open breeze,
Wind swirling round sprouting flowers,
Animals crying as they scatter and fly,
Moles digging tunnels to nowhere.

Mountains into the misty distance,
Ditches muddy and wet,
The leaves fall off the autumn trees,
Green, ripe grass shines towards the sunlight.

Trees left bare after autumn,
Winter starts to freeze all plants,
Animals start to hibernate,
Snow begins to fall.

**James Chase (11)**
**St Lawrence CE Primary School, Lechlade**


## Mother Nature

Mother Nature, so peaceful yet
Been eaten away from the way she was set.
And men do not seem to care
As they rip her beauty till it is bare.

She gives us our food,
We do not become clued
To how it was made,
But now it shall fade.

She gives us our material
And makes all our cereal,
She gives us our water,
And also our mortar.

**Stephen Watkins (11)**
**St Lawrence CE Primary School, Lechlade**

## Fairy

A garden fairy loves the air,
Her wings are so awfully fair.
She flutters around from leaf to leaf,
Through an enchanted berry wreath.

Cold snow fairy in the sky,
Shivering wildly, she's so shy.
Catching snowflakes on her wings,
Bouncing around like she's on springs.

Hot and sweaty summer fairy,
Wearing dresses, oh so flarey.
Jumping around, glitters' flying,
To do a flip she keeps on trying.

Fairies fly and leave a track,
Wondering whether to come back.

**Lauren Bullock (10)**
**St Lawrence CE Primary School, Lechlade**


## Seasons Of Joy

In winter the breeze is wild
And it screams like a child.
In summer it is hot
And I go swimming a lot.

August has falling leaves
And has windy trees.
In spring I see flowers
And I walk for hours.

**Isobel Stevens (11)**
**St Lawrence CE Primary School, Lechlade**

## Family And Friends

I love my family a lot,
My brother sleeps in a cot.
My best friend is my dad,
My baby brother is always bad.

When I go out to play,
Timmy brings toys out in a tray.
A boy next door always lies,
Will loves his pies.

When there are crisps about,
Henry gives a shout.
My mom is really funny,
I always want food for my tummy.

**Ben Fisher (10)**
**St Lawrence CE Primary School, Lechlade**


## I Want To Be A Dolphin

Dolphins are blue and grey,
Dolphins, they have their own say,
Dolphins like to jump and dive,
I want to be a dolphin.

Dolphins are kind and gentle,
To love them I must be mental.
They live so far away.
I want to be a dolphin.

Dolphins ride along with boats,
Imagine them in blue life coats.
With big, long fins they go so fast,
I want to be a dolphin.

**Megan Fidler (11)**
**St Lawrence CE Primary School, Lechlade**

## My Family

I like my family an awful lot,
They're the best, if I'm ill or not.
They will look after me when I'm hurt,
My family are the best.

If I ever have a fright,
They make sure I'm all right.
My family are the best.

**Matthew Knight (11)**
**St Lawrence CE Primary School, Lechlade**


## Bad Hare Day

Yesterday was a bad hare day,
Hares blocked up the motorway.
We beeped our horns but they wouldn't budge,
Until we hit them with toxic sludge!

The hares, they seemed to like it a lot,
Pretty soon they gobbled the lot!
Then it was all strange,
The hares they started to change and change!

They grew to the size of me and you,
They could even stand up too!
They reached for a jacket and put it on,
A flash of light and then they were gone!

I looked over at my friend Mike,
The hares, they stole his motorbike!
They all jumped on it and started to ride,
I tried to stop it, but missed its side!

We all set a trap to lure them in,
We had loads of carrots, enough to fill a bin,
They all came running to our trap,
We caught them all, and that's a rap!

**Joshua Richter (10)**
**Uplands CP School**

# A White Horse

I saw a white horse, as white as the moon,
She glistened like a shining star,
In a bright green paddock
She ran as fast as a cheetah,
Hair flying in the wind,
Tripped over a log on the ground,
Fell to the floor, *bang!*
The only thing that stuck out
Were her black eyes.

She got up in fright,
Swished her tale and started galloping.
Her eyes were as black as midnight,
Mane went down to her knees,
Hooves as black as coal,
She was as beautiful as a princess.
Mane looked like a white sheet,
As fast as the wind,
The only thing that stuck out
Were her black eyes.

She galloped over to me,
I stroked her, she ran away in fright.
Wild, I tell you,
Wild, wild, wild.
What was she doing in a paddock like that?
I opened the paddock gate,
She ran free, like never before,
Wild, wild, and forever more.
The only thing that stuck out
Were her black eyes.

**Jessica Vines (9)**
Uplands CP School

## Good Days

Christmas,
The best day of my life.
The best part is the presents,
Chocolate and all the food.

Easter
Is another good day,
Bags full of chocolate Easter eggs,
Don't eat too much.

Birthdays
Are good, I have cake and
Jelly and ice cream and a fab
Party with friends.

Holidays
Are fun and exciting,
What would I do without them?
They are one of the best things.

Pancake days
Are fun 'cause you flip and eat,
But not if they stick on the ceiling.

**Callum Webb**
**Uplands CP School**


## Looking For A Home

The wild cats roamed the streets
Looking for people to take them home.
Their big eyes were dark and green,
As they looked far into the distance,
Thinking about family and fish.
Cats watched through windows
And scratched on doors,
Watching families sat by the fire,
Having a feast and laughing,
Wishing they were in that picture.

**Jennifer West (9)**
**Uplands CP School**

## About A Car

A car goes *brum*,
A car goes *brum*,
Down the A4.

*Brum* a car goes up a mountain,
Smoking engine,
Panting and puffing,
That's how a car goes.

A car goes *brum* through a town
With great ease,
As silent as a mouse.

*Brum* a car goes across the sunset,
As a dark, bold figure
Purring like a great city cat,
That's how a car goes.

Down, up, through, across,
Exhausted and panting,
It stops as suddenly as a hunting cat,
That's how a car goes.

**Cameron Kyte (11)**
Uplands CP School

## Lion

Golden dust scatters in the wind
As the lion's paw hits the floor,
Claws like sharp knives,
Shining golden fur,
As light as the sunlight,
A mane like chocolate,
Teeth as sharp as daggers.
*Bang!*
A gun is shot.
The lion lets out a roar
Like a tsunami.

**Henry Cole (10)**
Uplands CP School

## Giraffe

He stretches his long, lanky legs out,
As his everlasting neck reaches the sky.
Munch, munch,
He's chewing on some gloomy, grassy, green leaves.

Then he senses danger.
Running gracefully, he tries to reach safety.
His big, brown, bold patches look like slate
Being left behind in the Serengeti.

Then a little while later,
He tries to find somewhere to sleep,
And he does,
Right under a sausage tree.

**McCoy Tinsey (10)**
**Uplands CP School**


## Elephant Poem

Elephants are big,
Elephants are kind,
Elephants are killed,
Why, oh why?

Is there a pleasure
In murdering them?
Help them, care for them,
Please don't kill them.

Elephants are mothers, fathers too.
What is the difference between them and you?

**Jade Riches (10)**
**Uplands CP School**

# The Strawberry Trifle Disaster

It was a beautiful, crispy night,
At that point the garden was in stunning state,
The stream layered with lights
And the strawberry trifle had not met his fate.

It was standing fluffy and crisp,
Frosty from the nippy winter's blow.
It looked like a gleaming moon covered in mist,
Ready to leap into a great show.

'Bring out the trifle, Jinny,' Mother cried,
So I did as I was told.
I was very bored with serving, so I sighed,
'You won't want to eat it cold.'

'Of course we will,' she cried once more.
'All right, I'll carry it out.'
*Bang!* I walked right into the door,
There were terrible screams and shouts.

As I looked, the trifle was not there,
Nor slopped on the floor.
I suddenly realised it had been in the air
And nobody was laughing, anymore.

'You idiot, Jinny.'
'You fool, Jinny.'
'You twit, Jinny.'
'You clown, Jinny.'

They were all shaking in custard and jelly,
Shouting and swearing rude things.
I felt like an idiot on telly,
And wished I could fly away with wings.

Even now I still feel terrible,
Though not getting told off,
Because I threw it on purpose.

**Ottilie Baker (10)**
**Uplands CP School**

## Football Crazy

Football is here for you to see,
Kicking the ball from you to me,
Best view ever, for he or she,
Come along now, you don't need a key.

Crowd is roaring,
Shouting and brawling,
People sing
Like a wild thing.

People eating
In their seating,
The whistle blows,
Up jump the rows.

Rushing forwards,
All towards
The toilet seats
And the canteen meats.

Everybody goes home at the end of the day,
Most people go home without a say,
Most people go home, but some people stay.

Out come the players in their posh new cars,
People are waiting behind the bars
To get the autographs from the stars.

**Ryan Thwaite (11)**
**Uplands CP School**


## Sadness

Sadness is like a dark night sky,
Sadness sounds like a sad groan,
Sadness tastes like bitter, sour lemons,
Sadness smells like the breath of someone shouting,
Sadness looks like dark fear,
Sadness feels like coldness surrounding you,
Sadness reminds me of a dark dungeon.

**Andrew Hartnell (10)**
**Watermoor Primary School**

## Secret Wood

There's a wood I go to with millions of flowers,
I count them growing by the hours.
I go there every single day,
They're always beautiful in every way.
There is only always ever me,
And the amazing flowers that I see.
They stretch over hills like giant colour-filled waves,
The pretty ones I will pick and save.
They give out wonderful and sweet smells,
Who knows how many stories this wood can tell?
I have never told anybody about the wood,
Or where it is even stood.
I sit there and have a cup of tea
Under a great big, attractive blossom tree.
You can taste the clear air,
Sometimes I just stand and stare.

**Megan Harding (9)**
**Watermoor Primary School**


## The Golden Eagle

Faster than Concorde, faster than a rocket,
Pierces the sky like a golden arrow,
Soaring swiftly up high and down low,
Over the hunters carrying their bows.

The golden eagle keeps a watchful eye,
Stares as the arrow sails through the air,
The eagle instantly drops down dead,
With a silver arrow right through his head.

Talons outstretched, lying on his back,
Lifeless body, blood oozing over smooth feathers.
The sun starts to set, to end the day,
The last ever sunset for this majestic bird of prey.

**Sarah-Jane Greenhalgh (10)**
**Watermoor Primary School**

## My Little Puppy

As I see Lily she bounds in my path, joyful to greet,
Leaping forward on her soft, padded feet.
She adores her comical, squeaky bone,
Barking excitedly with the ring of a phone.

Lily loves going for long, playful walks,
She teases the cat, but sadly got caught,
With a swipe of a paw and a loud angry hiss,
The angry little cat luckily missed.

Fortunately we caught her, but that wasn't the real matter,
It was that she broke my mother's new platter,
And a crystal glass or two, my mother's best set,
However she's lucky, because she's our favourite pet.

My mother is angry, but that soon will fade,
In licks and nuzzles she is nearly repaid.
Nobody can be angry at Lily for long,
She is as sweet and innocent as any spring song.

So all is now well with the world,
As Lily is asleep in my bed, tail curled.
Soft breathing and all is peace and quiet,
Until tomorrow, when again she will riot!

**Liam Tindal (10)**
**Watermoor Primary School**


## Snowstorm

Thrashing blizzards down in the town,
Freezing pipes, freezing cars, ice coming all around.

Howling wind, shattered glass,
Strong wind coming all around.

Creaking doors, power cuts off,
Cold icicles, dark clouds gather all around.

**Kes Wilkie (7)**
**Watermoor Primary School**

## Snowstorm

A freezing, shivery, cold snowstorm,
Squashy snow, wrap up warm,
Snowflakes dancing around,
Ice flakes melt in your hands.

Door shut, very chilly,
Warm tea,
Coffee please,
Quickly wrap up warm.

Squidgy, wet, cold snow,
People skating on the ice,
Snowflakes flowing down.

The sun is up,
The snow has gone,
Whoopee! My snowman Hola Hola!

**Katie Sandell (8)**
**Watermoor Primary School**


## Nature's Rage

Fire and lightning,
Burning and crashing,
Sparks fly
Throughout the inky sky.

Crashing and burning,
Wood turns to ash,
Hot embers glow,
Steaming droplets flow.

Crashing and burning,
Burning and crashing,
Is no more . . .
Plants crawl back to life,
Life begins again.

**Kieran Smith (10)**
**Watermoor Primary School**

## Snowstorm

Squishy, squashy, squelching snow,
Slippy, icy, sliding snow,
Shut the door or you
Get snowed in.

Big, blazy, blazing blizzard,
Swirling, twirling, squealing,
Shouting, howling loudly,
Close the door or you might fall in.

Freezing, buzzing, freezy wind,
Choking, moaning, moving twister,
Twister swirling, twirling, smoking wind,
Sucking, nibbling, eating wind.

A wild, breezy blizzard blowing,
Catching neighbours and gossip.
They stop and stare, quick, duck,
Everyone shouted, 'The snowstorm is coming!'

The bright, heavy snowstorm twinkled
Brightly, everyone looked and ran,
They were scared, didn't know what to do,
But go and bolt the door!

**Georgia Malone (8)**
**Watermoor Primary School**


## Love

Love is the colour of rose-red,
Love tastes like chocolate strawberry dip,
Love smells of angel perfume,
Love looks like strawberry-red love hearts and fireworks exploding,
Love sounds like singing angels,
Love feels like silk and smoothness,
Love reminds me of gossip.

**Molly Simpson (9)**
**Watermoor Primary School**

## Sounds I Like

Shadows swift past me,
Chattering under their breath.

Owls hooting, screeching,
Close in my ear.

Wolves' eerie howling
To the glistening full moon.

Foxes foraging for scraps,
Watching their ginger fur brushing in the air.

Rabbits hopping, bouncing,
Endlessly munching in fields.

The sound of stillness in the night,
Complete silence . . .

These are the sounds I like.

**Jonathan Sampson (10)**
**Watermoor Primary School**


## Darkness

Darkness is the colour of the midnight sky,
Darkness tastes like smoke in the air,
Darkness smells of death,
Darkness looks like nothing at all,
Darkness sounds like wolves howling,
Darkness feels like a rat's nose,
Darkness reminds me of loneliness.

**Georgia Voce (10)**
**Watermoor Primary School**

## Snowstorm

Cold snow blasting down,
Wind zooming round,
Wind so freezing cold,
Coming for me.

Screaming wind blowing,
Wind blowing really quickly,
Snow so cold you can freeze,
Getting near to me.

People running really fast,
Children running into their houses,
People shutting their doors and windows,
Getting nearer.

Houses, roofs covered in snow,
Tiles flying onto the floor,
People screaming, 'Help! Help!'
Getting nearer.

Cold snowflakes falling,
Icicles glittering,
Houses are covered in it,
Getting nearer.

Children screaming and shouting,
People's houses are covered in it,
Children's windows are covered,
Getting closer.

People screaming, as loud as they can,
Snow is falling faster and faster,
Ice is suddenly falling,
It's got me!

**Rachel Evans (8)**
**Watermoor Primary School**

## Snowstorm

The pointed icicles are prickly,
The snow is dashing down to the ground,
The freezing, icy, wet snow,
Sliding down the hills.

People running home to be in a safe place,
Houses swishing side to side,
Trees are covered in slippery snow,
Snowstorm on the hills.

The icy, dry snow,
Snowmen are falling on the ground,
The snow is horrible,
Going from the hills.

**Thomas Honey (8)**
**Watermoor Primary School**


## Lost

There's a town down the road
Where I haven't been before,
Nobody knows my name,
Or what I'm looking for.

Things may feel a little different,
I know that they won't miss the pain,
But I am going down the road
Where nobody knows my name.

I am feeling a little nervous,
Things will never be the same.
But I am going to keep going,
To the place where nobody knows my name.

**Toby Riddle (9)**
**Watermoor Primary School**

## Autumn

As I strolled out of the door, I heard the crushing of the crispy leaves,
I love the dewy smell of the fresh autumn air,
I love to feel the prickly shell of a spiky conker,
I love to feel the silk in a chestnut, all soft against my skin,
I love to eat the ripe, hard hazelnuts that fall from the almost bare trees.

Autumn is something I like
And I hope you like it too.

**Amy Gleed (9)**
**Watermoor Primary School**


## Love

Love is red, just like a heart beating,
Love is like an angel singing inside your head,
Love is like a sweet chocolate with almond nuts,
Love smells like a rose in the middle of a romantic date,
Love is like two hearts being together,
Love feels squishy like the cheeks of your boyfriend,
Love reminds me of my mum cuddling me really warmly.

**Tezhara Esteves (10)**
**Watermoor Primary School**


## A Victorian Match Girl

When icy winds go by
People never really need matches
I can see snowflakes fall down beside me.

I can hear silent footsteps in the snow.

I can smell fresh air and the coldness of winter
People strolling in the frozen snow.

**Molly O'Hara (7)**
**Woodchester Endowed School**

## A Victorian Rich Girl

A poor old match girl
With no money,
I want to help but the door is locked.
I can see bad things brewing,
Pick-pockets,
Fast and cunning.

I can hear the crackling fire
And a faint crying from outside.
I hate the sound of Mum and Dad bickering
Over who will close the curtains.

I smell delicious dinner on the table.

**Dorothy Scarborough (9)**
**Woodchester Endowed School**


## A Victorian Match Girl

Glimpse of rich families
Warm by their cosy fires.
People are shivering
While their coats are
Blowing in the wind.
I smell smoke from
Black and sooty chimneys.
I feel cold and terrified,
And most of all, freezing.
I hope to sell lots of matches
And have some money.

**Iona Lautieri (8)**
**Woodchester Endowed School**

## A Victorian Coal Miner

I'm a poor coal miner
I work all day
My name spells grime
I shove the coal here
I shove the coal there
My name spells grime
I'm a poor coal miner
I watch the stars go by
I watch the rich go by
My name spells grime
I'm a poor coal miner
I smell turkey as I pass houses
My name spells grime
I'm a poor coal miner.

**Tom Fickling (9)**
**Woodchester Endowed School**

## A Victorian Match Girl

Everyone wrapped up warm in big, soft coats,
With scarves and hats,
Arms full of shopping.
The cold fresh air is blowing up my nose,
And is tingling.
Litter blowing round and round,
Old bottles and cans rattling like old coaches.
I feel cold and lonely,
No one wants matches.
My feet are getting colder and colder.

**Alexis Hall (8)**
**Woodchester Endowed School**

## A Victorian Chimney Sweep

Black bricks as dirty as can be,
A little light peeking through the top,
A powerful smell coming from down below,
Getting ashes in my eyes.
Chattering everywhere!
Out in the street, down below,
Everywhere!
I feel as gloomy and as heartbroken as can be,
My only hope is to be the master of the house.

**Paul Sampson (8)**
**Woodchester Endowed School**


## A Victorian Match Girl

A basket full of colourful matches,
There are people with packages in their hands,
A lighted match burning in the dark,
People talking and horses trotting.
I am cold and no one looks after me.

**Louise Mullen (8)**
**Woodchester Endowed School**


## A Victorian Coal Miner

I see a shadowy cave in front of me,
I smell black, chalky coal being
Shoved through the narrow tunnels.
I hear rusty carts creaking and cracking.
I feel spiky rocks cutting my painful feet.

**Milan Alden (8)**
**Woodchester Endowed School**

## A Victorian Coal Miner

A wooden dusty cart full of dingy black coal.
The clash of a brown glinting pickaxe scraping down the coal.
I smell the hot stuffy air whistling up my nostrils.
I feel that I could run away because my back aches endlessly.
I hope that one day I will be at home in front of my hot smoking fire.

**Freddie Waldon (8)**
**Woodchester Endowed School**


## A Victorian Match Girl

I see people buying matches
Why not me?
I can hear blowing gates,
Rattling window panes and rattling newspapers around me.
I can smell burning wood in a richer home.
I wish that was me.
I feel uncomfortable in my bones.
It's horrible.
Staying up with no money.

**Emily Radcliffe (7)**
**Woodchester Endowed School**


## A Victorian Pickpocket

Silver shillings waiting for me to rob,
A shimmering pocket watch in Prince Albert's pocket
The smell of revenge on the local bobby
Wheels of a horse-drawn carriage loaded with gold
Money jangling in Victoria's handbag
I can smell another rob coming on
I dream of being rich.

**Toby Redding (9)**
**Woodchester Endowed School**

## A Poor Victorian Child

Big-headed rich children telling me I'm poor.
People stare as I skip with old parcel string.
The smell of burning bread wafting from the baker's.
More match girls selling sweet, beautiful flowers.
The clanking of pennies in a poor child's bucket.
The howling of the wind, opening and closing shutters.
Frightened of falling to my death.
Concerned about going home 'cause Father will beat me
I hope things will be better in the morning, and I'll have a
                                                nice fresh start.

**Isobel Lewis (8)**
**Woodchester Endowed School**


## A Victorian Match Girl

Busy people running past
The smell of fresh air
Cross people shouting
Trying to get the work done
I feel very sad.

**Ben Jones (7)**
**Woodchester Endowed School**


## A Victorian Match Girl

I can see children running past
Throwing rubbish on the ground
It is freezing
Nobody buying matches
I smell rotten fish on a stall
Dirt being kicked at me.

**Tommy McInerney (7)**
**Woodchester Endowed School**

## A Victorian Chimney Sweep

*I see* black burning soot and red and black bricks
    A bright shining light from the top of the chimney
*I smell* burning fire from the fireplace
    And smoke from the chimney
*I hear* the crackling noise of the
    Fire underneath my black soot feet
*I feel* frightened and scared.

**Luke Daniels (9)**
**Woodchester Endowed School**


## A Victorian Rich Child

I see all my precious toys gleaming in the sunlight
I can smell the strong scent of the wet paint on the saddle
                          of my rocking horse
Soon I could go galloping across the fields
I hear my mother and father shouting at the servants
Like Queen Victoria and her guards
I feel my mother and father coming up to see me
To say we're going to get more money
You can have anything you want except friends.

**Jack Lister (7)**
**Woodchester Endowed School**


## A Victorian Chimney Sweep

Darker than words can say
The chimney is not a pleasant place
The scraping as it peels off your skin
Like rind off an orange
Black soot powder stuffing up my nose
Blood dripping from my bleeding cuts
I wish my master would do this.

**Sam Weller (7)**
**Woodchester Endowed School**

## A Victorian Chimney Sweep

I see;
Nothing but pitch-black soot,
Just sitting there in lumps,
Waiting to infect my sore eyes,
No sign of life,
Not even a spider,
Just me.

I hear;
My master below snoring,
His two spoilt children playing,
This isn't my day!

I feel;
Sick,
My arms and legs
Have
Friction burns
And I'm tired.

I wish;
I were dead
Because I know there is no other life
In store for me.

**Thomas Little (8)**
**Woodchester Endowed School**


## A Victorian Rich Child

Horses and ponies galloping
Trains are swaying and tossing
Rocking horses swinging
Train set rolling on its sparkling wheels
With steam coming from its engine
Maid brings toast and sizzling bacon.

**George Staniforth (9)**
**Woodchester Endowed School**

## A Victorian Coal Miner

I saw the overflowing cart being hauled down the track
I could smell the earth and coal mixed together
I could hear the flickering of the candle next to me
I felt sad and lonely
I could see the gas lamp on the wagon being pushed down the tunnel
I could smell the wax of my candle
I could hear the crunch of the coal and the wheels together.

**George Drake (8)**
**Woodchester Endowed School**


## A Victorian Coal Miner

I see people dragging all the heavy coal
I smell the dirty coal in the coal truck
I hear the noise of the trucks dragging on the rusty tracks
I am losing my strength pulling all the coal along
I feel cold in this mine.

**Isaac Fearnley (7)**
**Woodchester Endowed School**


## A Victorian Coal Miner

I see coal miners working in the mines.
Dirty and desperate to get home.
I smell dirty black horrible dust going past me.
I hear the heavy cart being pushed by a tired coal miner.
I feel like a black and dirty monster.

**Molly Leech (7)**
**Woodchester Endowed School**